THE THEATRE OF THE MIND

Cover art by *Jane A. Evans*

THE THEATRE
OF THE MIND

Evolution in the Sensitive Cosmos

HENRYK SKOLIMOWSKI

*This publication made possible with
the assistance of the Kern Foundation*

THE THEOSOPHICAL PUBLISHING HOUSE
Wheaton, Ill. U.S.A. / Madras, India / London, England

The Theosophical Publishing House
306 West Geneva Road
Wheaton, Illinois 60189

Published by the Theosophical Publishing House,
a department of the Theosophical Society in America.

Library of Congress Cataloging in Publication Data

Skolimowski, Henryk, 1930-
  The Theatre of the mind.

  1. Evolution—Addresses, essays, lectures.
2. Theosophy—Addresses, essays, lectures.   I. Title
BP573.E8S56   1984   299'.934   84-40165
ISBN 0-8356-0588-4 (pbk.)

Printed in the United States of America

Acknowledgments

My bountiful thanks to Maurice Ash and the Trustees
of Dartington Hall for their forthright generosity in supporting my stay at Dartington where these illuminations
were written; to the Findhorn Foundation which invited me
to give a series of seminars on evolution, and thereby
caused me to think at large; to the late Margaret Callaway
for the invaluable secretarial assistance and other
forms of help; and to Shirley Nicholson for her superb
editorial guidance.

Table of Contents

Introduction
As a Personal History

The Vital Oxygen of Philosophy

Why should anyone be interested in philosophy
nowadays? Because without philosophy we are crippled.
Philosophy is like air. We must have it in order to breathe.
Our air may be clear or contaminated. But we must
breathe all the time. Philosophy is a form of oxygen which
supports all our thought. We always do have some kinds of
philosophy as the backbone of our thinking, whether
we know it or not. Nowadays, alas, it is so often a crippling
philosophy, at best indifferent to the ends of life, and
not infrequently supporting the idea of life as a ruthless struggle for the survival of the vicious.

The call for a new philosophy is really the call for a
new foundation of our being, for a new air which we can
breathe not through our lungs but through our minds,
hearts, and souls. This is what great philosophy has
always been: vital oxygen to our minds and hearts which
makes our souls alive.

The main body of this volume is made of short essays
which I call illuminations. I hope that the content of these
essays redeems my claim to call them *evolutionary* illuminations. Each is short and succinct, without, I hope,
being dogmatic. I chose terseness of expression in
order to bypass the pompous verbosity of many present
discussions which belabor the argument and arrive
at no conclusion. We are only faintly acquainted with the

1

mysteries of the human mind, and we do not know for sure whether it comprehends best through lengthy discursive arguments, or whether it is most attracted and compelled by crisp poetic expressions which convey the essence in a striking manner. For the present volume I opt for conciseness.

In a sense I have attempted to write a series of upanishads for our times. Upanishads are those immortal Hindu stories which deal with the human condition and the cosmic condition in a most sublime manner. This is not to say that I have attempted to write immortal stories. Rather I have tried to take up those great human and cosmic concerns, which are present in each of us, and give them an expression in our language, see them reflected through our problems and dilemmas.

Before I present my illuminations, I shall share with the reader the story of my philosophical quest: where I have been, what I have found or not found; why past philosophies are deficient and beyond mending; and also why we must have a new philosophy so that we do not forgo the most precious heritage of the human race. Books are written by real people. But so often we have the impression that they are written by disembodied minds. Our personal history *is* our mind. I have attempted to reconstruct the vicissitudes of my mind to let the reader share the sources of my inspiration and the causes of my agonies.

From Warsaw to Oxford to Los Angeles

You may not be able to surmise from the illumination that I am a product of four cultures and at least three different systems of thought. Born in the pre-war Poland, I experienced for the first nine years of my life the perfectly ordinary bourgeois life in Warsaw. Then a cataclysm came—the 1939 war, followed by the horrors of German occupation. A different culture emerged—the culture of survival, of heroism, of cooperation, of trust in one another vis-a-vis the vicious occupant. I learned that there are circumstances when one has to fight against

2

unfair odds, indeed against impossible odds. One has
to fight even if one's life is imperiled. Such was the
imperative of living during those years under the German
occupation. Heroism was a form of transcending the
degrading conditions of life. The unwritten motto was: if
they will not let us live in dignity, we can at least die
with dignity—fighting them. So at twelve I found myself in
the Resistance movement, smuggling illegal pamphlets
under the eyes of the Germans. At fourteen I took part in the
1944 Warsaw uprising. Many people, particularly in
the U.S., think that there was only one uprising in
Warsaw—the Jewish one in 1943. Yes, we had witnessed,
in the other part of Warsaw, the heroism of the Jews and
saw the Ghetto systematically burned and destroyed
section by section, in the full knowledge that it was the
Jews today, us tomorrow. A year later it was so. During the
1944 uprising some 250,000 people were killed and
85 percent of the city turned to ruins and ashes. How you
survived, you do not know. You do not think obses-
sively about survival. When people die around you, it
becomes natural to assume that next time it may be your
turn. Cowardice does not pay in such circumstances.
You have to stand up and be counted, even if you are
a boy of fourteen.

The war experiences help you to acquire a certain
distance from life. When your family lost all its possessions
twice, including the house in which you lived—and you
felt lucky to have escaped with life—you are not likely to
think that material possessions and material security
are all there is to life, for you know that material security is
no security at all.

More importantly, when you see people dying daily
on the streets in defense of their dignity and freedom, you
experience some ultimate situations in life; then you are not
likely in your later life to go with the prevailing winds
and compromise endlessly for the sake of expediency.
You are not likely to be twisted around by such persuasions
as "Don't rock the boat." In brief, it was in those dark
days of the German occupation that the foundations of my

non-conformity were laid; and the conviction was born that you must go on searching and fighting in order to give witness to the most noble part of the human condition in us.

In my early twenties I was much under the influence of the stoic moral philosophy. Stoicism was the right reply to the crazy circumstances of the early 1950s in Poland. At one time I knew the entire little moral treatise of Epictetus (The Manual) by heart. I must have felt a great moral affinity with him. Somehow I sense that the moral teachings of the stoics have stayed with me throughout my life.

Now another "culture" in the form of Marxism was imposed on Poland, first gently in 1945, then ruthlessly in 1950. Those times were quite a spectacle. It was in a sense like living in a theatre, the theatre of the absurd, one should add. It was by and large a make-believe reality. For the sake of some great and stupendous future in which the classless society would run its idyllic course, and in which all would be happy and fulfilled, a systematic distortion of truth on a gigantic scale was taking place. People pretended that they believed what they were told, yet they didn't. However, after having gone through the motions for so long, they finally did not know whether or not they believed what was being constantly repeated. The situation was made more opaque even by constant insistence that the present was not important. What was important was the distant, stupendous future.

We were thoroughly skeptical of all the ideological nonsense imposed on us in the form of various Marxist dogmas. It would be a mistake, however, to assume that all of Marxism was rejected as worthless rubbish. In spite of its crudities and limitations, there was a core of idealism in Marxism which many found irresistible. Thus Marxism became—if only subconsciously—a challenge to our imagination and the call of great ideals which claimed one's attention and one's altruism. It is for this reason that Marxism seduced so many. The larger ideals lurking behind Marxism, though distorted by it, gave

4

us a sense of responsibility to history and to the future. Those larger ideals ultimately convinced many that to have a mission is not foolish but indeed noble.

Thus I was inculcated with the sense of appreciation of history and the sense of responsibility for the future. This I consider a souvenir from the Marxist culture of the 1950s.

Then came the Oxford interlude, when I was given a fellowship at St. Antony's College to write a D.Phil. dissertation in philosophy. In 1959 when I first arrived at Oxford, linguistic philosophy was at its peak there. The sense of confidence that Oxford was the mecca of philosophy was all-pervading.

The mystique of Oxford has always been great. In the late fifties, it was at its height. One sensed conviction in the air that the real revolution in philosophy had been completed and we were its inheritors. I came from the background of Polish analytical philosophy, and when I compared its achievement with that of the Oxford School, I could not see why Oxford felt so superior. The funny thing is that at Oxford nobody is treated as a special person, let alone a great man. At a place where everybody is a somebody, nobody is anybody.

Still, to write a dissertation in another language is difficult enough. To write one to satisfy Oxford's fastidious demands, especially in philosophy, was a bit of an ordeal. But one had to cope. I had no desire to return to the ideological nonsense of Marxism in Poland. The situation was slowly deteriorating in the 1960s and the whole climate in Poland became increasingly oppressive.

The lesson of Oxford was more disturbing than illuminating. I learned that if we pronounce our utterances with confidence and dazzle others we can put across all kinds of nonsense, although our grounds may be shaky indeed.

The other lesson I learned at Oxford was that linguistic and analytical philosophy was really thin and in a sense fatuous. A conviction was dawning on me that Western philosophy had found itself in a cul-de-sac. I felt

5

very strongly that something was wrong with the enterprise which at first promised so much but, as the time passed, simply did not live up to its promise.

My time in Britain was not all frustration and disillusion. Far from it. It was an exciting period of discovery. One of the discoveries was Karl Popper and his philosophy, which I will discuss later.

In 1964, after Oxford, I went to teach at the University of Southern California in Los Angeles. This was a culture shock. Indeed I found myself in quite a different culture, although the language and the system of values were seemingly the same as in Britain. I will reveal the impact of this new culture on me while describing changes that occurred in my outlook in the late 1960s.

From Plato to Linguistic Philosophy to Philosophy of Technology

So much for the cultures that have formed me—I will now go into the texture of this book after a few words about the systems of thought that shaped my imagination and horizons and are implanted in these pages. The first was that of Plato. In my late teens I was devouring all the great literature of the world. In due course I stumbled upon Plato. At first I read him as a poet and a writer. However, I was gradually sucked in and spellbound by his marvelous mind. His discourses on the importance of Form as shaping and molding everything, read at times like fiction. But what a marvelous and fascinating fiction it was! It actually *explained* everything. I became a philosopher through Plato. To this day I do not know whether his philosophy is one great, fantastic fiction—the greatest fiction ever written to haunt and dominate human imagination—or whether it is an attempt to describe reality in depth. The philosopher in me took a long time to emerge. Before it did, I was meandering through other avenues of life. But the enigmatic smile of Plato was with me all the while.

6

In 1950 I found myself entering the Department of Geodesy at the Warsaw Institute of Technology rather than philosophy at Warsaw University. The reason was simple. I wanted to study philosophy, and not the history of the Bolshevik's party and other Marxist teachings. It was in the early months of 1950 that the Marxists took over. In order to avoid the ideological nonsense, I decided to study engineering. "Equations do not explode," said Bertrand Russell. I told myself that engineering cannot be a subject of ideological manipulation. Thus I spent five and a half years at Warsaw Institute of Technology, acquiring two degrees in the process. Furthermore, I taught surveying at the same institute for another five years. The study of engineering was difficult for me as it went against my grain. But then it was a difficult period for everybody. My studies of engineering were to prove beneficial years later when I found myself pursuing the critique of technology and the entire Western civilization. Because I was an engineer, my credibility proved to be greater, and my arguments were regarded with more consideration than those of others who did not go through the grinding mill of scientific/technological education.

After Stalin's death in 1953 the situation started to improve in Poland. I found myself attending lectures and seminars at Warsaw University in the Department of Philosophy, mostly lectures given by "pre-war" philosophers who were previously on the index. Soon I allied myself with Tadeusz Kotarbinski, who was a great mind recognized for his philosophical accomplishments the world over, but also the moral conscience of Poland. Under his influence my allegiance to Plato began to wane. Kotarbinski's was an altogether different kind of philosophy—minute, logical, analytical, mostly concerned with highly sophisticated semantic issues. Moreover, it was a form of materialism, albeit of a very refined semantic variety. The doctrine was called *concretism* or *pansomatism*, as nothing but physical bodies were recognized as primary objects of one's ontological and conceptual universe.*

It is strange how pliable our minds are. We, Kotarbinski's pupils and followers, were rather a distinguished lot from various philosophical predilections and with different temperaments. Yet we all came to accept his doctrines, not because they immediately struck us as true or illuminating, but rather on the moral authority of our teacher. Here was a man recognized all over Euope for his philosophical achievement, recognized in Poland, moreover, as a man of impeccable moral authority. Since his philosophy represented the finest achievement of human thought at the time, who were we, his students, to question him? So we submitted. Though I am reluctant to say so, it was a submission to authority, not to truth or the inner voice. This form of submission to the analytical authority of the masters is still going on in Anglo-Saxon universities, producing devastating moral and human consequences. The minds of students are made as sharp as razors, but their human horizons can be as limited as those of zombies.

The fruit of my studies with Kotarbinski was an M.A. in logic awarded for a thesis in the philosophy of mathematics, and of course a thorough knowledge of the language and the problematique of analytical philosophy. Since Kotarbinski was known in the West, I had fewer difficulties in obtaining a fellowship at Oxford than I would otherwise coming from a Communist country. I was one of the first research students from Poland, and the curiosity among the British about life in Poland was considerable. This is in contrast to America. When I arrived in the U.S. in 1964, people seemed to know better what was going on in Poland than I did; they had their stereotypes well in control of their minds. It struck me over

---

*For the detailed description of Kotarbinski's philosophy, and of the whole Polish analytical school, see: H. Skolimowski, *Polish Analytical Philosophy*, Routledge and Kegan Paul, 1967.

and over again that the American culture is much more stereotyped than the European culture—the result of mass media.

As I said earlier, I was not impressed by the achievement of analytical philosophy at Oxford. Tired of its aridity, I moved to London towards the end of my stay in Britain and started to participate in Karl Popper's seminars at the London School of Economics.

Popper's seminars and his philosophy were a wonderful liberation from the narrowness, and in fact tediousness, of analytical pursuits. More than that, here was a man who could *think* under your very eyes. I experienced the excitement of philosophy being created before me in Warsaw with Kotarbinski and Ajdukiewicz, but not at Oxford. Popper's capacity to think relentlessly had some undesirable consequences, namely when he sometimes kept on thinking without having a sufficient basis in knowledge.

However, the fact remains that in the power of ideas Popper was second to none, and he encouraged the spirit of search in others. The ambience was intense and creative, with sparks flying everywhere. Philosophy was taken seriously. By doing philosophy one was doing something important. Thomas Kuhn's book *The Structure of Scientific Revolutions* is universally hailed as a breakthrough. Popper was a real breakthrough. Kuhn only continued and refined the idiom. In a sense Kuhn has stolen the glory that was due to Popper.

Popper's philosophy is a form of critical realism. The role of criticism was elevated to an almost sublime and sacramental position. All intellectual activities were seen as a process of trial and error in which relentless criticism of all positions is of key importance. Above all, Popper's was a philosophy of science which also provided the rules of the praxis of science—how to do science in order to arrive at new and original results. At the same time, science was considered the pinnacle of human achievement, the most important attainment of the human mind.

How do you start intellectual endeavors? You set up a

conjecture (which may be inspired by anything—no privileged sources of knowledge) which you call a Tentative Theory (TT¹). Then you follow with a relentless criticism of your own theory, which is the process of Error Elimination (EE), so that you can arrive at an improved theory TT^2 as the result. The whole scheme put together reads: $TT^1 \rightarrow EE \rightarrow TT^2$. The power of Popper's scheme in the reconstruction of the history of science and in the actual practice of science is undoubted. Moreover, starting with a very few simple insights, Popper was able to develop a whole new epistemology (see especially his *Conjectures and Refutations* of 1963).

Yet when one asks large and deeper questions, such as what this philosophy has to say about the human condition, about society, about religious and spiritual questions which have haunted the human mind from the time immemorial, then one finds Popper's philosophy curiously mute. For this philosophy is another version of 20th century rationalism, another cognitive reconstruction of the world—mainly through the conceptual tools of science, historically and dialectically reformulated.

In all those purely cognitive and rational reconstructions, the wholeness of man is reduced to his neo-cortex, to his intellection, to the product of his abstract brain. Popper took a great step forward. In comparison to logical positivism, his dialectical and open-ended philosophy was liberation. However, the rigidly cognitive mold by which he wanted to restrict all philosophy makes Popper's philosophy of limited value in the long run and vis-á-vis life's larger problems. In later years, I found Popper's philosophy disappointing. In the mid-1960s, however, Popper was an inspiring antidote to analytical philosophy.

Applying Popper's methodological program, I first liberated myself from the narrow confines of analytical philosophy, and then I liberated myself from the dogmas of Popper's philosophy itself. This was to happen in the U.S. when I realized that science may be the most powerful *intellectual* force we as a society possess. I noticed, however, that it was technology that was

10

determining the course of society and, in a sense, shaping human destiny. My philosophy of science had become philosophy of technology. But then technology could not be confined to the cognitive realm. It had to be seen as a social force and also a determinant of our individual existences. My philosophy of technology had broadened itself to become also philosophy of man and philosophy of culture. I also realized that it was not sufficient to analyze the defects of the Western intellectual tradition, particularly the post-Renaissance times, and search and search to find "where we have gone wrong." One had to go beyond more criticism, beyond cataloging the defects of Western mind and Western culture. One had to go on to develop a new philosophy, an alternative cosmology. Without embarking on the path consciously, this is what I found myself doing in the 1970s in the U.S.

Seeing the Cracks of Western Culture

I arrived in Los Angeles in the fall of 1964 to teach at the University of Southern California. The shock of transition from Oxford to Los Angeles was at least as great as the one from Warsaw to Oxford. The year 1964 was the twilight of the Kennedy era. The right kind of optimism still prevailed and people were inspired by larger ideas. The epoch of universal prosperity seemed to be around the corner. The technological euphoria was high.

While the technocratic optimists were making all kinds of bombastic and dogmatic predictions about the future, a moral revolution was taking shape which was to shake the world. It was preceded by a deep economic recession in 1967, when yet another agonizing process was going on at the same time, the war in Vietnam, which was to leave deep scars on the nation's psyche. The gradual disenchantment with the outcome of the war turned into despair and the feeling of horror.

Then came the flower children revolution in 1967-8. There was an electric effect when girls of the age of fifteen, sixteen, or even seventeen, handed over a single flower

11

with a smile. There was something inherently beautiful in the act. Deep down we felt that they were telling us something significant in a symbolic way. The deeper cords of one's inner self reverberated.

Then came the hippie revolution. The hippies were not so symbolic. They were explicit, and sometimes brutally so, in condemning the status quo and the whole of society for its moral rottenness, for its hypocrisy, for its bringing about a world of unprecedented alienation, for its total inability to live as it preached—a happy and fulfilled life. They were relentlessly questioning: "What has gone wrong?" No one had any comprehensive answers then. Let us not delude ourselves: the fundamental challenge to the heritage of post-Renaissance Western civilization posed by the late 1960s still remains unanswered.

I lived within walking distance from all the ferment that was happening around Sunset Boulevard, where things were bubbling and brewing. I was fascinated by the scene, which was verging on fantasy. I listened to the intensity of new voices, to moral indignation, to scraps and bits of new visions. I participated in their discussions. I didn't have satisfactory answers either. Yet I knew that things did not happen by themselves. There must have been some turning points which put us on wrong trails. What were they? Who was responsible for them? This was puzzling and disturbing, for if you trace back the steps of Western society for the last three or four centuries, you find logic and consistency. Each step followed coherently the previous ones. The 17th century, which was the beginning of secularism, gave rise to the 18th century which became (or at least it so called itself) the Age of Enlightenment, which in turn gave rise to the Industrial Revolution, and then to the technological society of our times. And what was our guiding image and moral inspiration? Progress, which nobody dared to question until the late 1960s. In the name of progress we were impoverishing ourselves spiritually, and in the name of progress we produced over 50,000 nuclear war heads. The logic of the process could not be seriously challenged, for there was consistency. Besides, the implementation of the ideals of material progress brought about considerable material gains. Yet something had gone wrong. The young people knew it instinctively.

You could, of course, dismiss the cries of the hippies and the flower children as whimpers of a bunch of confused youngsters. Many did; many still do—teaching and preaching worn-out ideas as if they had real validity. I tried to listen to the young people, reason with them. I said to myself: if this is a bunch of confused kids, why cannot we—with our reason, knowledge and clarity—give them satisfactory answers? In truth, we couldn't. I also listened to positive visions and new philosophies proposed by the hippies. They did not amount to much. Upon deeper reflection I knew that the search had to go much deeper, right to the very foundations of our thinking, which has become somewhat diseased; right to the very foundations of our morals, which are too often corrupted by our expedience and shortsightedness.

Here then was a fundamental challenge to a philosopher: to examine the basic assumptions of our civilization, to find out (specifically) whether they are indubitable truths, or at least inspiring and sustaining myths; or whether, perchance, they have not become unwarranted dogmas manipulating our individual lives and dwarfing our larger horizons. It was the latter, by and large, that I found to be the case.

In the course of my journey into the foundations of our technological culture, I have also discovered that we Western people—almost the bulk of Western society—want to live in delusion. When we look deeper into our inner selves, we often *know* in our hearts and also in our minds, that many beliefs by which we live are simply false. Yet we go on with the game of appearances. Why? Because we also know that this process of systematic delusion is in our self-interest as a materially privileged people who live comfortably and often at the expense of others. So too often we blur the edges of our consciousness and talk about our economic necessities while the inner voice tells us something else.

The continuous process of self-delusion, living with half-truths and sometimes obvious lies, is at the heart of the sickness of the whole West. Communist countries are not excluded. I have mentioned earlier that they have perpetuated and perfected their own game of self-delusion, in the name of some glorious future. In brief, no one can live in grace and at the same time wallow in affluence at the expense of others. Grace excludes waste and self-delusion and making mockery of one's own life.

The Mirage of Objectivity

Grace is easy to postulate but difficult to justify. The critic may say that when we postulate grace we deal with intangibles, whereas our world is made of tangible things; our lives are lived in concrete and tangible dimensions. In our world of science and technology we must have an *objective* justification for whatever we do and whatever we think. And the critic may continue: the people who are aspiring to radical alternatives and alternative world views may be well meaning, but they cannot sufficiently justify their views to convince us, the believers in rationality and objectivity. You have to be objective and rational.

Having been raised in the rigors of analytical philosophy and then of philosophy of science, at first I accepted the pronouncements of the critic as undeniable truths, at least as the principles necessary for the function of the mind that considers itself intelligent and enlightened. Yet in the course of years, I reflected on the principles of objectivity and rationality—how they manifest themselves in our system of knowledge and how they function in our lives, that is, when ruthlessly adhered to. I came to the conclusion that those two firm pillars of Western knowledge and of Western mind are wobbly and altogether suspect.

The public listens to the white-coated scientists when

14

they pontificate about the objectivity of science and the impeccability of their scientific results and tends to accept these as a new gospel. The public has no access to the frailty of scientific results. For one who has been close to the scientific mind and who has critically reflected on the value and place of objectivity in human knowledge, the situation looks different.

When we start to inquire into the status of objectivity, it will not be unreasonable to ask: how *objective* is the principle of objectivity itself? Is it a principle of nature? It is not. It is a principle of our mind. The quest for objectivity is a predilection, a preference of some minds. There is nothing in nature or in human knowledge (before you assume that all knowledge must be objective) to compel you to accept this principle, except the social pressure of conformity. Nature does not know what objectivity means.

There are some still deeper problems with objectivity. Of late the New Physics has been telling us a fascinating story, namely that *we never look at nature objectively.* We simply are unable to do that. If objectivity means being free from the filters, limitations, propensities, and frailties of our mind, then we never are objective in this sense because we filter and process *everything* we perceive, everything we think about, always.

Thus we live in the *participatory* universe, not in the objective one. The notion of objective knowledge independent of our minds is an absurdity, according to the proponents of the New Physics. Furthermore if we look at the actual behavior of creative scientists at their best, we are struck at how idiosyncratic their thinking is. They are simply not objective. They are human and messy. In their thinking, they follow inner hunches, intuition, and often use unorthodox and even weird methods. A marvelous description of this complex creative process is given in Crick's and Watson's book *The Double Helix.*

I had various occasions to witness how fictitious and frail the principle of objectivity is while I was interacting with scientists on their own grounds. There was a big international conference in San Francisco in 1977. It was attended by a most impressive array of minds from some 100 countries. One symposium was devoted to recombinant DNA research, a very hot subject at the time, and still a highly controversial one as it has to do with the possibility of genetic manipulation of human beings. The scientists in favor of the research wanted to sweep aside all objections because the imperative of research was most important to them. They didn't care about the possible consequences. What they cared about were the new results. The critics suggested that we should go slowly and look before we leap. The spectacle was rather bizarre. Here was a galaxy of first-rate minds, in a free country, at an international conference especially set for free inquiry, and they were as parochial and bigoted as parish priests in the Middle Ages. And this is not an isolated incident. Such things, often in the name of objectivity, do happen.

What were the arguments and reasons that so agitated my fellow scientists during our San Francisco meeting? One was: In pursuing DNA research we are actually beginning to tamper with the nature of life itself. In order to tamper with the nature of life in a fundamental way, we have to have wisdom and moral responsibility; in my opinion we have neither. And this argument has been quoted many times over in the literature pertaining to DNA research. But the scientific community did not want to hear it.

My criticism of the scientific ethos is the result of a close scrutiny of the inadequacies of the primitive philosophy which science often assumes as its basis (scientism): but also the result of watching closely—and with astonishment—the abuses of reason and human intelligence by the scientific community, often under the banner of objectivity. (See my further discussion of objectivity in Chapter 23.)

All of this can be found in almost any competitive community. Universities are competitive communities par excellence. Instead of being temples of learning and centers of excellence, they are the anthills of rivalry, full of "human masks whose substance is fog."

Let me conclude this section with some general remarks. The pursuit of objectivity has brought some undoubted benefits in our explorations of the physical universe. However, the principle of objectivity must not be treated as a deity because, as is the case with all human products, it is a very frail thing. If I were to say that objectivity has become a pernicious dogma, many would raise their voices in alarm and accuse me of being anti-science, so I shall not say this. I shall maintain, however, that the nobility and the freedom of our minds require that we liberate ourselves from any straightjacket, be it the dogmas of religion or the dogmas of objectivity. We are free, authentic beings. Our minds are marvels of creativity and spontaneity capable of going to depths undreamed of by the principle of objectivity. In chasing the mirage of objectivity we have tried to apprehend a chimera, alluring in its shape, which, however, does not belong to the human universe.

Searching for a New Conception of Man

Life is always messy, always ambiguous. At certain periods of history it is more ambiguous than in other periods. We are living in such a period now. We Western people have too often made ourselves repositories of hypocrisy. Deep down we know the crookedness of many of our ways and at the same time accept them because they are in our selfish interests. At the same time, however, we search for new paths—of sanity rather than hypocrisy; we search for new ways and paradigms which are sustaining to life, which would facilitate symbiotic relationships with all other beings rather than exploitive ones.

What do you do, then, when you are a philosopher in the midst of a culture that is breaking apart? You may wish to—or indeed be compelled to—face the realities and problems of your times, the agonies peculiar to the human condition of your times. As for myself, I did not seem to have any choice but to be a witness of our times, the witness who at the same time tries to find new paths.

So I listened to the flower children. I listened to the hippies. Some of them were quite extraordinary people who had insight and courage, who in a sense were able to cross into another culture—which was not yet there. However, they did not have enough substance and perseverance to make the vague outlines of this new culture into something permanent. Part of the problem was that they did not go deep enough into their own foundations. They did not re-examine the whole value system with sufficient care. They often naively assumed that good intentions and groovy life style would *automatically* transform their consciousness and the social consciousness, and this alone would bring about the new culture.

One still could ignore the whole scene (and most did) and tell oneself that this bunch of confused kids and meandering dropouts could not possess more wisdom than the great philosophers of the past. And so, one could go on (as most did and still do) teaching and preaching old doctrines now completely worn out and divorced from life.

While searching for the roots of our problems and agonies, it became clear to me that the fault did not lie in our stars but in our philosophies, in the visions that the great philosophers of modern times impose on us. Let no one underestimate the power of philosophers. They are the real rulers. They are responsible for our myopias and distortions, and also for delegating the power to the machine. Their visions compelled us to mess up our present world. I am quite aware of what I am saying, namely that the philosophers are responsible.

Francis Bacon, Galileo Galilei, René Descartes are the renowned philosophers of modern times. We revere them for their discoveries, yet, strange as it may sound, what they found in nature was simply not there. Bacon pronounced that knowledge is power. But nature does not care whether knowledge is power or not. Instead, nature is a seamless web of forces which nourish and sustain

18

each other, including us.

Galileo said that the book of nature is forever open to our gaze, but in order to read it we must learn the alphabet in which it is written; the language in which it is written is that of mathematics. Yet *the book of nature is written in living forms* not in mathematical formulas. The formulas may at best reveal to us the skeleton of living forms. But then the skeletons are stripped of life, are not these *living forms* themselves.

Descartes suggested that in order to understand the nature of our problems, and indeed the nature of the world at large, we must break every dilemma into its constituent parts; divide and subdivide until we arrive at atomic problems which are so simple that we can easily handle them with the tools of our analysis. Yet the strange fact is (and we all know it) that nature is made of *patterns* and *wholes* which are beyond analysis, for if you break these patterns and wholes into their constitutive parts, you no longer have patterns and wholes. At best, you understand the constitutive components.

The three men I have singled out—and they are by no means the only architects of the modern Western mind—have tricked us into accepting their visions as if these were the truth about reality. I must emphasize this point: what they have shared with us was not what they *objectively discovered* out there, some principles which were deeply laid in Nature, but their visions which they imposed on us. Acting on these visions, we made them into a reality. Once we began to look at reality through the lens of these visions, we started to perceive and sort it out accordingly. We started to mold the structure of the world and then of our lives in the image of these visions, in the image of the metaphors they project. We started to reject or at least leave aside anything not accommodated by these new outlooks. Hence we have ended with a one-sided picture of the world and a crippled image of ourselves.

The mechanistic metaphor started to dominate our entire horizon. We have attempted to fit everything into a structure which we assumed to be a mechanism moving according to simple, deterministic laws. Paradoxically, within ourselves we have always known that this is not true of our lives. The consequence of this process of the progressive mechanization of the world was the deracination of man, who became uprooted and cut off from the sources of his natural energy: living beings, living habitats, understanding of the cosmos at large. On another level, and after a time, this deracination led to frustration and anger, to human beings turned into jelly-fishes, oozing, and stinging when touched.

> Of all you have done in the past
> You eat the fruit
> Either rotten or ripe.
>   T. S. Eliot

The utopias and visions of the 17th century philosophers are now bearing rotten fruit. This was one of the conclusions at which I arrived while attempting to understand our predicament, particularly in context of the hippie revolution. Looking back at the last two centuries I could now see how the visions and insights of Newton, Hume, Locke; then of La Place, Diderot, Condorcet, and Comte; then of Marx, Engels, and Lenin, all belong to the same mold, predominantly materialist, secular, anti-spiritual. They were all different expressions of the same ideology of secularism. They preached salvation here and now, on earth. And what of the soul? What of Nature, of man's spiritual quests? Let them wither. They aren't important, they declared.

Action never guides itself, for then it is a stupid action and occasionally violent. The adulation of practicality and efficiency of modern industrial society is but a consequence of the mechanistic reading of the universe based on materialism. The practical wisdom of our times which despises philosophizing is, ironically, itself a fruit of a philosophy—though rather barren and shallow.

Once you have identified the sources of rot, you cannot go on denouncing positivism and scientism forever.

Exorcising the spooky ghost of Descartes from morning to evening doesn't solve the problem, although it may give some aesthetic satisfaction. You have to build alternatives, you have to attempt to work out new world-views. If the whole matrix is wrong and beyond mending, you have to create a new matrix, a new paradigm, not only for science but for the entire empiricist world-view.

Already in the early 1970s it became obvious to some of us that the ecology movement was fumbling, as it did not go deep enough into the conceptual foundations underlying our thinking and acting. In the early summer of 1974 a symposium was organized at the Architectural Association School of Architecture, in London. The subject was "Beyond Alternative Technology." I was one of the four symposiats, and I used the occasion to outline for the first time some principles of Eco-philosophy, which at this time I called Ecological Humanism. In a nutshell, I argued the following:

  1 - The coming age is to be seen as the age of steward-ship: we are here not to govern and exploit but to maintain and creatively transform for the benefit of all beings.
  2 - The world is to be conceived as a sanctuary. We belong to certain habitats; they do not belong to us. They are the source of our culture and our spiritual sustenance. We must maintain their integrity and sanctity.
  3 - Knowledge is to be conceived, not as a set of ruthless tools for atomizing nature, but as ever more subtle devices for helping us to maintain our spiritual and physical equilibrium.

Ecological Humanism, which incidently is far removed from traditional concepts of Humanism, and specifically from the anthropocentric rationalist-scientific Humanism of the 19th century, in due time gave rise to my book *Eco-Philosophy, Designing New Tactics for Living*, published in 1981. One of the main inspirations for the book, and also for this volume, was Pierre Teilhard de Chardin. His view on the phenomenon of man, combined with

21

new insights of astrophysists such as John A. Wheeler, open for us altogether new vistas on the prospects of man.

As I was examining the traditional conceptions of man (throughout the text for *man* read: man and woman, simply the human being), I found man pitifully mis-represented by these conceptions. There is Aristotle's celebrated concept of man as a rational animal. This conception of man was supposed to add to our stature and dignity, as rationality was in a sense enshrining our nobility as human beings. And what have we done with the nobility of rationality? It has sometimes become a blind instrument of exploitation. The rational man has too often become the technological fixer, the organization man, the not uncommon research scientist who unashamedly sells his shining intellect to the military industry so that even more lethal weapons can be produced. In short, we can no longer identify the essence of man with his rationality, for this rationality has turned out to be a terrible two-edged sword.

There is the definition of man as Homo Faber, the tool maker. This too is full of traps. Homo Faber in our times is turning into a Frankenstein monster who has not enough sensitivity, not enough moral sense, to know what to produce and why. The original premise of technology was different: the amelioration of the human condition. Now, if we look at man as the tool-making animal, we will notice upon closer scrutiny that before we could make ourselves into tool-makers, we had to first make something of our minds. Thus a deeper reading of the conception of man as Homo Faber simply reads: man the-mind-making-animal.

Then there is the conception of Homo Ludens which suggests that play and playfulness of our nature characterize our essence. And what have we done with the idea of man as a playful animal? Our tendency is to suffocate this man through the vulgarity and triviality of modern mass entertainment. We have become consumers of the entertainment industry, which more often than not feeds us with vulgar kitches and in the process contributes to the atrophy of our sensitivities and sensibilities. Therefore, this conception of man will not do either.

In searching further I concluded that perhaps the best characterization of the human being is that he is a self-sensitizing animal, or simply the sensitive animal. For it appears to me that the range and power of our sensitivities uniquely determine our status. This definition allows us also to connect man with the entire stream of evolution and treat both as the continuous process of refinement and emergence of ever new sensitivities. Evolution is a self-sensitizing process. The more sensitivities it acquires, the richer it becomes. *We live in the sensitive cosmos.* In the common parlance, the scope of our sensitivities is usually, but not justifiably, narrowed to so-called soft aspects of our being, to aesthetic and moral sensitivities. I want to argue that *every single capacity we possess is a form of sensitivity*, including the capacity for abstract reasoning which may be called the logical sensitivity. Sensitivity is the subject of my first illumination, and the theme runs throughout the book.

1

Sensitivities, Our Windows on the World

What is most important about man is that he is a
sensitive being; that he is endowed with sensitivities; that
via sensitivities he is making his evolutionary ascent.
Man is, in short, self-sensitizing, that is, self-transcending
and self-perfecting. New sensitivities are new windows
which enlarge the horizons of our world. They are also
the vehicles by which we carry on the evolutionary
journey and through which we make ourselves into more
human and more spiritual beings.

When the first amoebas emerged from the primordial
organic soup, they were victorious because they acquired
a new sensitivity enabling them to react to the environment in a semiconscious manner, which was the beginning
of all learning. For learning is a capacity, a sensitivity,
to react to the environment and its conditions in a feedback
way. The glory of evolution starts when organisms begin
to use their capacities, thus their sensitivities, in a
conscious and deliberate manner to further their well-
being.

From the organic soup via the amoeba to the fish;
from the fish via reptiles to primates; from the primates
to man—this has been a continuous and enthralling story
of the acquisition and refinement of ever-new sensitivities.

When matter started to sense and then evolved the
eye as the organ of its new sensitivity, this was an occasion
of great importance. Reality could now be *seen*, could

be articulated according to the power of the seeing eye. No eye to see, no reality to be seen. It is the eye that brought to reality its visual aspect. The existence of the eye and the existence of the visual reality are aspects of each other; one cannot exist without the other. For what is the seeing eye that has *nothing* to see? And what is the *visual* reality that has never been seen?

The seeing ability of the eye is a form of sensitivity through which we articulate reality around us. Seeing is one of many sensitivities. They are all products of the articulation of evolution. But they are not just passive repositories of the evolutionary process. Through them we mold, apprehend, and articulate what we call reality. There is no more to reality (for us) than our sensitivities can render to us. Sensitivities are articulators of reality. To say it once more: the emergence of every new form of sensitivity is a new window on the world.

With new sensitivities we articulate the world in new ways; we elicit from the world new aspects. The power of sensitivities is the power of co-creation. No aspect of reality imposes itself on us with irresistible force; we take it in and then assimilate it if, and only if, we possess an appropriate sensitivity that is capable of processing this aspect of reality for us.

The power of creation is the power of articulation. When painters such as the Impressionists begin to see reality in a new way, they invariably articulate it in a fresh way. Without a novel articulation there is no new seeing. Every new creative act is a new act of articulation. Creation is the process; articulation is the product. This is also how nature goes about her business, by endlessly articulating. And such is the story within the human universe: by acquiring new sensitivities we acquire new powers of articulation. Thus we acquire new powers of creation. Sensitivity, therefore, holds the key, not only to our understanding of evolution, but to the understanding of ourselves. To summarize: we are bundles of quivering sensitivities. What is most important about man is that he is a sensitive being.

Let us probe this question a bit further. Are we confusing thinking (and knowledge) with this vague stuff called sensitivity? No. Thinking is a form of sensitivity. It is a form of seeing with an immediate recall of past experiences stored in our evolutionary layers. Paradoxically, thinking is not the kind of faculty that we often imagine it to be. It was not inserted into us at a certain stage of our evolution as a gift from somebody who said, "Now cerebrate." Thinking nearly always occurs within a larger framework of our experience, and of the experience of the species, and this experience makes thinking much more than mere cerebration. Thinking is one of the many threads of which the tapestry of our sensitivities is made; it is only one aspect of our evolutionary endowment. And this endowment is often mind-boggling. If you reflect on it you will find that the laboratory of the world is all contained in us; the entire chemistry of the cosmos is circulating in us. The chains of energy are transformed into life. Two grams of energy into one gram of life? What is this energy which becomes life and then becomes consciousness? Consider the relationship between chemistry and consciousness. We know that it exists. If we starve the brain of oxygen, loss of consciousness follows. But this is really a tiny facet of what is there, of what takes place. We carry within ourselves the laboratory of the world and in a sense the entire knowledge that has ever existed. Yet we have so little awareness of it. The epistemology of life has to be created so that it can perform this great task awaiting it, which is to excavate the cognitive layers of evolution. This is not a philosophical fantasy. We so often resort to the knowledge stored in the layers of our evolution, and on occasions we become aware of it as well.

In explicating the concept of man as a sensitive animal, I have found that I was articulating a new conception of knowledge as well as a new conception of mind and of reality. The rudiments of these conceptions are spread throughout the text of these illuminations. The concept of man as a sensitive animal—as the being that makes his

evolutionary ascent by increasing the scope of his sensitivities—provides us with a clue for many puzzling
dilemmas with which the discursive, logical mind cannot
deal, and with which our empirical knowledge is ill at ease.
Why did the flower children and the hippies get it right
in spite of their relative ignorance as compared with the
learned? Because their sensitivities, and particularly moral
sensitivities, were sharp and acute enough to inform
them—via this subtle process called the feedback of the
inner being—that things in the outside world could not be
right if they produced such devastating social, ecological,
and existential consequences. There is no mystery here, no
resort to magic or the supernatural. There is only a
deeper sense of *understanding* how things are connected
in our deeper layers when we listen to the beat of our
hidden sensitivities, and how they respond to all the
myriads of inputs that filter through from the outside
world.

Looking at the human being as the field of quivering
and alert sensitivities enables us to explain some other
phenomena which are puzzling to the physical scientist
and to the whole paradigm of knowledge based on the
physical. It has been consistently noticed in all cultures
that so-called simple people, that is, the ones without
formal education, often find a way to the heart of the
problem and offer insights and solutions that are astonish-
ing to the learned. Those simple people—because they do
not possess "sufficient" knowledge—are not supposed to
come up with those insights that surprise the learned;
yet they do, often making mockery of the learned. How is
this possible? They resort to deeper sensitivities which
reside in the sanctuary of their inner being. This also applies
to intuition and especially the "feminine intuition," out
of the depth of which, somewhat miraculously, correct
answers emerge without thought, as it were. This again
astonishes us. But it would not if we were properly
attentive to the full repertoire of our being. Actually those
flashes of intuition do not astonish us when we are fully
fledged human beings. They only astonish the physical

27

scientist who wants to reduce everything to the physical and the logical. Not even that: they only astonish mediocre scientists. The great ones are friends with their intuition, cherish and nurture it.

The phenomenon of man as the field of expanding sensitivities also sheds a new light on the experience and aspirations of mystics, seers, and poets. We hear from them that we are capable of reaching the infinite. Consider Blake: "If the gates of perception were unclogged, every object would be seen as it is: boundless." Aldous Huxley speaks in similar vein in his celebrated book *The Doors of Perception.* Sacred books of the past inspire us to believe the same thing: we are infinite—if we only open ourselves sufficiently.

As much as I love the inspiration and fire of Blake and Huxley and many of the sacred texts, they are misleading us. The matter is more subtle and complex. It would be too easy to open those windows or gates if we already possessed them. It is not even a matter of unclogging them. *These windows or gates are often not yet there.* We have to create them first. We create new windows, we erect new gates of perception, by creating and nurturing new sensitivities. And this involves our entire being in a steep climb against the odds of ordinary reality.

We shall see every object as it is—boundless—only when we *become* boundless, when our sensitivities become infinite, when we are one with godhead.

Now let us return to the evolutionary ascent of man as seen through the prism of unfolding sensitivities. We now have a simple, unifying perspective. In the evolutionary journey the first elementary perceptions—the amoeba crudely sensing its environment—give way to another form of sensitivity eons of years later—human illumination. Philosophy, art, religion, as well as knowledge including science, are forms of human illumination, refined forms of sensitivities evolved over time.

Through sensitivities evolution is articulated.

Through sensitivities the mind of the human being is created.

Through sensitivities the scope of our humanity is delineated.

Through sensitivities matter is transformed into spirit.

All thinking is light which we shed on the objects of our understanding. This light, when it illumines life, becomes reverence for life. Reverence for life is a form of human sensitivity towards it; at the same time it is a form of thinking about it. Thinking so conceived can be seen throughout all traditional cultures. Plato's fusion of Truth, Goodness, and Beauty is a manifestation of it.

In the making of symbols we have found another way of augmenting ourselves. For symbols have facilitated a new, important stage of our evolutionary articulation: by developing symbolic codes we have brought art, religion, and philosophy to fruition; in the process we have articulated ourselves as social, cultural, and spiritual beings.

Truth, goodness, love, and beauty are vehicles of our sensitivity. They are an outgrowth of our early 'natural' sensitivities which, through symbolic transformations, become instruments of illumination and, furthermore, of spiritual articulation. What we call 'spirituality,' 'the religious feeling,' 'the sacred,' and 'the divine' are all expressions signifying an enhanced sensitivity, an enhanced capacity of the individual to react to the world and to transcend the limitations of matter.

To define the human being as a sensitive animal, as one who forms himself through the acquisition and enlargement of his sensitivities, is to pay homage to the openness of man's future and also pay homage to the attainments of evolution. The right concept of man is one which acknowledges all man's past attainments but which, at the same time, makes man open to future refinements, to the acquisitions of the power of consciousness far beyond anything we have so far attained. It is not only, and not so much the capacity for, rational thinking or the capacity for making tools that we shall have to cultivate in order to become more than we are at present; we shall have to evolve new sensitivities, some of which are yet undreamed of, some of which are given to us in rudimentary forms such as telepathy, but all of which signify and delineate our being in the sensitive and self-sensitizing cosmos.

Let me finish with some general remarks about the new philosophy that has been thrust upon me. Philosophy was born of the condition of grace, and it must return to the condition of grace in order to start fulfilling its historic mission. It is difficult to define the term *grace*. Yet deep down we all know what it means, analytical philosophers not excluded. I am appealing to their sense of grace as well.

For something truly tragic has happened to our civilization in terms of the loss of the soul, in terms of the loss of the inner self. Where is the light we have lost in the darkness of the satanic mills? Where is the human will we have relinquished to the mute computer? Where is the spark divine we have exchanged for the refrigerator full of plastic goods? Yes, the light is there, inside us; the will is there although in the state of slumber; the spark divine is buried but still alive. We can reactivate them, but only through the total reconstruction of the cosmos we shall choose to live in.

The evolutionary illuminations that follow attempt to outline an alternative future based on a new reading of evolution. The aim is to provide a unity between the cosmos and man in which human purpose is congruent with the élan of evolution, and human meaning is restored as part of a larger meaning.

When I write about evolution, deep down I know that it is evolution that is writing about itself through me. I have been pondering over the mysteries of evolution for a number of years. Yet I cannot resist the feeling that it has been evolution itself that has been collecting these ideas over eons of time for me. How could it be otherwise? Then in 1980 I was invited by the Findhorn Foundation to lead their week-long seminar on contemporary theories of evolution. This proved to be a momentous occasion, during the course of which many ideas became unlocked and burst out into distinctive patterns. The result is this volume.

What Bergson, Whitehead, and Teilhard de Chardin grasped gropingly and intuitively—the creative nature of evolution—emerges as an imperative of our times, the imperative for a human and humane survival. It is not uncommon that ideas of promise need 50 years to mature before they are absorbed by a culture and incorporated into its new purpose.

The old war between science and mysticism is coming to an end as science increasingly gravitates towards the ineffable and mysticism seeks rational justification. In fact, the two can now be seen as different aspects of the same spectrum: human knowledge and human experience. Rational mysticism, which is one of the main threads of these illuminations, offers itself as a new form of reconciliation between the rational and the ineffable. Rational mysticism may strike some as a contradiction in terms. Yet both rationality and mysticism are inherent parts of our human heritage.

Language is a reality that enables us to transcend the reality of rocks and of other physical bodies. Language is a reality that, at times, enables us to transcend itself—all the particular and fragmentary meanings contained in particular sentences, and then, as if through the glass darkly, we gaze at something incomparably deep and radiant—the reality of our inner selves as part of the harmony of the cosmos. This is a state in which Eastern mystics proclaim that Atman and Brahman are one. I cannot hope that these illuminations will bring the reader to this domain, which is essentially beyond language. But I can hope that they may help the reader in the journey toward this realm whose name is Enlightenment.

2
Science and Evolution

Evolution precedes science. The process of evolution
has generated the process and the phenomenon called
science, not conversely. We must emphasize this, for we
often behave as if evolution were *created* by science, and
indeed at the mercy of science. We should acknowledge
this: the pursuit of science has made evolution conscious of
itself. Science made us aware that evolution takes place.
Then we discovered that we are a part of this evolution;
we are that part of evolution that is conscious of itself. Thus
evolution begets science, while science makes evolution
conscious of itself.

Evolution is a *frame* concept, a totality concept. It
outlines the boundaries and sets preconditions for other
things; it defines them but is not itself defined by them.
Since it is a totality concept it cannot be easily con-
veyed by the language of science, which deals with *parts*.
The context determines the nature of our discourse, be it
scientific or otherwise. Science finds evolution to be
a "scientific" phenomenon because it *a priori assumes*
evolution to be so. Since evolution outlines the boundary
for all phenomena, we can find in it the scientific and the
irrational, the aesthetic and the cosmological, the social
and the human; we can find in it every part and aspect
of what we consider our heritage and our surrounding
reality.

Evolution is hidden behind every precept of science.

Therefore, no experiment in molecular biology or bio-chemistry, indeed no scientific theory or any specific finding, can be considered decisive about evolution as the total process. Let us emphasize: *each* scientific theory and *every* particular experiment derives its meaning and receives its validity from a larger context, otherwise known as the conceptual framework, which itself is a part of knowledge, and which in turn is part and parcel of the cognitive evolution of man. To reiterate, evolution cannot be reduced to science, for it provides the *context* for science. It is in this sense that science *follows* evolution and not the other way around.

Today science cannot be the arbiter of all questions concerning evolution, for it is an enterprise which has its own problems which are more grievous than we usually suppose.

Science is about *reality*. It aims at *truth*, that is, at descriptions that are true. It relies on evidence that is supposed to be *indubitable*. These are the premises of science; the premises on which the whole enterprise rests and from which it derives its validity. Science, no doubt, is a many-splendored thing, but of late it has suffered an identity crisis which also affects the entire Western culture.

Now although it is *assumed* that science is about reality, scientists are at present reluctant to maintain that their theories and statements *are* descriptions of reality. For example, what is the reality of the ultimate subatomic particles?

Although science is supposed to be about truth, scientists at present are reluctant to talk about the truth of their theories and utterances. Also the conviction is no longer as strong as it once was that the kind of evidence science provides is indubitable and cannot be doubted.

Under the impact of its own discoveries, particularly in subatomic physics, science finds reality to be increasingly elusive. Why? Because the ultimate constituents of matter which physics has searched for with such diligence and conviction seem to avoid the grasp of physicists and to recede further and further as they are approached.

33

The situation is both extraordinary and agonizing. In deciphering the structure of matter, we went deeper and deeper and identified ever more "elementary" particles, until we arrived at the point of such profusion of these particles (over 300 of them identified!) that the whole structure, which was to be rendered lucid through them, dissolved. This is by no means a poetic metaphor but the description of the state of proliferation of entities which do not explain that which they were meant to explain. Instead of arriving at the ultimate truth about the structure of matter and the nature of elementary particles, physics has created a conceptual and ontological confusion on an unprecedented scale. An eminent particle physicist has recently mentioned: "Physics is in a terrible state." And a general question emerges: in what sense, if any, are these "elementary" particles *particles* at all? Is there any real and not just metaphorical sense of the term *particle*? The whole notion of empirical reality—or physical reality—if it is to be grounded in those elementary particles (conceived as the fundamental constituents of matter) is tottering.

If our reality becomes elusive and beyond our grasp, and, if moreover we are in the situation in which the observed and the observer merge inseparable, then this is bound to affect our notion of truth. Truth is to be a faithful and unequivocal description of reality which is objectively "out there" and independent of us as observers. However, if reality becomes elusive and no longer independent of the observer, how can we have unequivocal and objective truths about it? Let us rephrase the point: When reality becomes elusive to the point of becoming intangible —as is the case in the realm of ultimate elementary particles in which the observed and the observer merge inseparably—then the process of matching our descriptions of reality with reality itself becomes extremely difficult if not impossible. We no longer have firm, "objective" reality "out there" which we "photograph" in our theories and in our language. Whoever respects elementary logic must accept these conclusions.

34

Let us look at the problem of evidence in this context. If reality is elusive, then our truth about it becomes at best tentative; and our evidence concerning this reality is something less than unshakable and unequivocal. For how can we have evidence which is indubitable and unequivocal if the very notion of empirical reality itself is in question? Now, we are not saying that reality has *ceased* to be empirical, but only that we do not know any more what *empirical* means.

We now have revolutionary new insights into the nature of science: the realization that all knowledge is tentative, that physical reality can be comprehended only within contexts, or conceptual structures, or paradigms; that scientific rationality is not foolproof but something that is often question-begging; that the ultimate objective basis of the physical world is somehow dissolved in the myriad of subatomic particles. These have profoundly changed our outlook on science and the kind of world it attempts to describe. These insights also affect, for they must affect, our notion of evolution and particularly the scientific approach to evolution.

Recent developments in science have simply invalidated its older mechanistic, objectivistic, deterministic image. Yet this old image dies hard. I have recently had the honor of talking on evolution, within a broad philosophical framework, to a distinguished group of scientists and philosophers. I was told in the discussion that it is to science that we must look for *correct* views on evolution. I was told, in short, that science knows best. The whole spectacle was rather bizarre, for on the one hand I tried to show how science has changed during the last seventy years and how different it looks now as compared with its early dogmatic, infallible, deterministic position. On the other hand, there came a rebuttal based on the reaffirmation of an older view of science: objective, static, seemingly infallible. The debate over my views was symptomatic of our times and our confusions. We know that science is no longer an objective, firm, pyramid-like edifice, but something much more elusive, mysterious, fascinating, far-reaching. Yet when we talk about science in the context of our civilization, we invoke the image of an infallible deity. The sad truth is that the new outlook on the nature of science has not yet become a part of our new outlook on the world; it has not even penetrated deeply enough in our schools to prevent us from being brought up and educated, still, within the regime of 19th century science.

Science has recently transcended its mechanistic model. The story of science transcending itself is a magnificent manifestation of evolution's chief modus operandi—ceaseless and continuous transcendence. It is now up to us to allow our minds to transcend their mechanistic confines and other deterministic trappings in order to create a world view—which at least would match recent horizons of science.

3
Mapping Out Theories of Evolution

The number of theories of evolution is overwhelming. The first acquaintance with them produces headaches and confusion rather than illumination and understanding. These various theories sometimes clash with each other and sometimes not as they direct themselves to different problems and indeed to different realities. We can map out the various theories of evolution in relation to the problems they attempt to answer. There is the whole spectrum, starting with scientific theories and ending with "cosmic" theories. Within the spectrum we shall find overlapping epistemological, philosophical and eschatological theories of evolution (see diagram).

Scientific theories of evolution are concerned with such questions as: How did matter evolve? How has life emerged? What is the molecular/genetic structure of life? Can we explain all of life by means of basic physical/chemical constituents? What is the role of emergent qualities (characteristics) in the formation of new species? The disciplines within which such questions are raised and discussed are molecular biology and evolutionary biology, but also comparative zoology, cytology, ethology, etc. If we really look into the matter with perception, we realize that whenever scientists address themselves to larger questions concerning evolution, such as the origin of life, they subtly but invariably move away from their specialized scientific domains. They enter larger

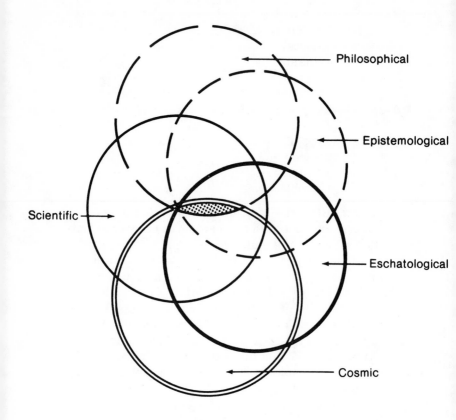

Philosophical

Epistemological

Scientific

Eschatological

Cosmic

waters. They simply *speculate*.

Epistemological theories of evolution (*epistemology*
is another name for the theory of knowledge) are concerned with more general problems such as: What are the
mechanisms that are specific to evolution? What kinds of
systems are there in nature? What is the role of brain/
mind in evolution? What is the specificity of the knowledge
which is peculiar to our understanding of evolution?
What is the relation of this knowledge to strictly scientific
knowledge? Among the treatises specific to this branch
of enquiry could be mentioned Gregoire Nicolis and

38

Ilya Prigogine, *Self-Organization in Nonequilibrium Systems*; Eric Jantsch, *The Self-Organizing Universe*; and Gregory Bateson, *Mind and Nature, a Necessary Unity.*

The epistemological problems of evolution have always attracted the attention of scientists, of philosophers, of theologians alike, as they have to do with the origin and becoming of things. The epistemological problems of evolution are perhaps at the center of our current concerns. They have more 'respectability' than other extra-scientific problems of evolution: they try to establish *structures* which are rigorous or semirigorous and thus appease our quest for the precise and the definitive.

Philosophical problems of evolution investigate such questions as: How can we evaluate our knowledge of evolution? What is the nature of evidence in evolution at large? What is the meaning of the term *evolution*? What is the connection between our understanding of evolution and the meaning of human life? There is a large area of overlap between scientific, epistemological, and philosophical problems of evolution. Any problem or theory of evolution that goes beyond the strictly scientific may be termed philosophical. Thus the most significant discourse on evolution is invariably philosophical, whether we are aware of it or not.

Eschatological problems and theories of evolution are the most emotionally charged (eschatology is the discipline or the branch of enquiry which is concerned with ultimate goals and ends of human life). Among eschatological problems are: what is the meaning of evolution within the human context? and conversely, what is the meaning of human life within the context of evolution? Is the meaning of human life inextricably woven into the meaning and the tapestry of evolution and, if so, what is the ultimate sense of both? Are we responsible for carrying on the burdens and glories of evolution? If so, why? The purpose of all religions (including secular ones, such as Marxism) is eschatological—the redemption of the individual. Whether we seek this redemption in a transcendental heaven or here on earth, the idea of this redemption is nothing else but the crystallization of human meaning. In present times the phenomenon of evolution —self-transforming and endowed with spirituality—is the context for this meaning; evolution is so often seen as the path leading to this redemption.

Cosmic theories of evolution are closely related to the eschatological ones but, as we would expect, their scope is still broader and expressed in such questions as: What is the meaning of the human destiny vis-a-vis the cosmic destiny? What is the meaning of the cosmos and the place of evolution in it? What is the role of the cosmic (or universal) Christ in evolution? Does mysticism and the entire body of esoteric teaching offer any special knowledge or insights into the cosmic questions of evolution? Are there two separate realities governed by two separate sets of laws, so that we cannot understand what it is all about until and unless we have grasped the meaning of the cosmic law?

This brief review of the differences in the nature of evolutionary problems should make us aware that it is useless to try to answer some of the large eschatological questions (such as what is the meaning of man's life vis-a-vis the meaning of evolution) through narrow precepts and confined categories of science. And it is dangerous to try to use eschatological categories for strictly descriptive and scientific problems, such as mechanisms of reproduction.

It is prudent to realize, however, that the variety of theories of evolution responds to the variety of aspects of our being. It is also prudent to realize that there is an area of overlap where all our concerns meet: the focal point of convergence which signifies the unity of man amidst his diversity.

Given the spectrum of evolutionary theories, let us ask ourselves, which inquiry is more legitimate: probing into the structure of DNA as the carrier of genetic material, therefore capable of shedding light on the evolution of life; or probing into the meaning of Omega Point which, even if it is only a hypothesis concerning the possibilities of evolution, is so enthralling and sheds so much light on

40

our past and present? *Who* can say that one question is more legitimate than the other? From the standpoint of our search for enlightenment, they are both legitimate. But their legitimacy derives from different kinds of questions and different realms of knowledge. Curiously and significantly, different though they are within the spectrum of all knowledge, both these questions are wonderfully speculative. There can be no question that the research concerning genetic information as carried within the genes is highly speculative: we can never see *information* as grafted on any gene. This is all based on imaginative conjectures. We must not hail imagination when it concerns scientific matters and condemn it when it concerns ultimate stages of our evolutionary journey, for this would be sheer hypocrisy. The inquiry into the meaning and extensions of Omega Point is among legitimate quests of the human mind and of human imagination. Our journey of knowledge is not finished. What questions will be considered as legitimate in some distant future may surpass our wildest dreams.

4
Of Right Understanding

To understand the nature of science is to understand the
nature of its growth. To understand the nature of evolution
is to understand how it transcends itself.

To understand the nature of evolution is the beginning
of wisdom.

Evolution is all. And nothing is beyond it. *Nothing* is
beyond it. It signifies the process that has generated it all. It
generates, but is not generated. It is thus the prime mover
of things. What was before evolution, we do not know.
Once it started, evolution is the process and the product; the
point of departure and the point of arrival.

To have a right view on evolution is not only to possess
important knowledge; it is also to possess right forms
in which to behold our experience. To choose the right
theory of evolution means to choose the right perspective
on reality, to possess the right kind of model for interaction with reality, which also means the right kind of
model for one's own life.

To possess and behold a right theory of evolution is
to understand the rhythm and the dialectics of evolution.
But it also means to weave ourselves into this rhythm and
breathe with it. To breathe the rhythm of life is to be at one
with it, to be healed by it. Thus the right knowledge
of evolution is self-healing in the sense of enacting life in a
right way.

But evolution is not a simple thing. Its dialectics are

perplexing. Evolution moves in harmonies which are continually being re-established, which also means they are continually breaking. We are part of this breaking harmony that constantly re-establishes itself. The joy of becoming is perpetually accompanied by the pain of leaving our older shells, which means our older selves. To understand the dialectics of the harmony of evolution is to be able to see that things and harmonies are broken, not without a reason, but in order that new things can be created, so that the process of transcendence can go on. Transcendence is the key to the understanding of the dialectics and harmony of evolution; thus evolution itself holds the key to understanding ourselves. To be, in the evolutionary sense, is to continually transcend.

5
Teilhard and Soleri

One cannot but express one's admiration for the mind of
Teilhard de Chardin (1881-1955), who almost single-
handedly elevated evolution from the dreary domain of
social Darwinism to the iridescent realm of matter
transforming itself into spirit on its way to Omega Point.
The courage of his mind in following relentlessly the design
that struck him as right, and the tenacity and skill in
weaving the multitude of phenomena and processes into
one structure of great complexity and staggering beauty are
among 20th century intellectual achievements second
to none. Nobody who writes about evolution in the second
half of the 20th century can bypass him, even if they
disagree with him. Though grudgingly, more and more
scientists are accepting his contribution.

Why has Teilhard received a rather rough treatment
from the scientific community? Because he posed too much
of a threat to the whole framework and ideology of science.
Oddly, the hostility (or at least nervousness) over Teilhard
was not based on the fact that his ideas could be shown
to be false within the universe of science. His ideas
clearly were of the kind that could neither be proved nor
disproved by science; therefore no scientific refutation
was possible.

It may be claimed that in his messianic zeal to make
evolution a universal deity, he overreached himself and
claimed more than he could justify. But which philosopher

44

of importance hasn't? His main treatise, *The Phenomenon of Man*, is not a scientific one, although Teilhard claimed it to be. Nor is it essentially a theological treatise, although Teilhard bends over backward to accommodate his view to the prevailing Catholic orthodoxy. It is quintessentially a cosmological treatise—a new way of articulating the cosmos. Pope John Paul II called Teilhard a great phenomonologist of the cosmos, and he was right.

I said that Teilhard almost single-handedly transformed our *vision* of evolution from the pedestrian to the celestial. This is not quite correct. He had a worthy predecessor in the French philosopher Henri Bergson (1859-1941) without whom Teilhard's venture would have been hardly possible. Interestingly enough, Bergson was born the year Darwin's famous work *On The Origin of Species* was published. But with Bergson we enter a new epoch in our views on the creative nature of life. The two most powerful concepts of Bergson's philosophy are *creative evolution* and *élan vital*. Nothing could characterize his system more succinctly than these two concepts which form a bridge between Darwin and Teilhard. Bergson's major work, *Creative Evolution*—elegant, lucid, inspiring—was published in 1911. In 1913, Teilhard read it and this proved to be an inspiration for life.

Bergson's influence on Teilhard was greater than Teilhard cared to admit. The spirit of creative evolution permeates Teilhard's vision through and through. Pugnacious rationalists of the early part of the 20th century, including Bertrand Russell, accused Bergson of irrationalism and of trying to resolve too many problems at one stroke. Indeed, in *Creative Evolution* Bergson tries to resolve at once problems concerning evolution, mind, matter, memory, time, and free will. The philosophical idiom of the time was edging towards sober, small, minute, logical analyses. Bergson was quite clear that "philosophy can only be an effort to dissolve again into the whole." This insight Teilhard wholly incorporated into his thinking.

Teilhard also contended, with Bergson, that inanimate matter lends itself perfectly to abstract intellection,

whereas when we enter the realm of the living "we must adopt a special attitude towards it" and examine it with a different sort of vision than that of physical science.
The acquisition of this other *special attitude* towards the living comes very hard to all of us, conditioned by physical, objectivist science. The chasm is sometimes so great that scientists say (and no doubt mean it) that they do not know "what you are talking about" when we mention this *special attitude towards the living*. The process of raising our consciousness so that it will be responsive to the call of Reverence for Life (about which Schweitzer was so passionate) has to do with the acquisition of this special attitude towards the living. This attitude may be the single most important element in our understanding of evolution as a creative process; it is also a prerequisite of empathy and compassion—as modes of understanding.

Whatever influence Bergson might have had, Teilhard's opus is singularly his own. He is his best exponent. *The Phenomenon of Man* is not only a great adventure of the mind, it is also an ABC of *evolutionary* thinking. I shall not attempt to summarize it here. Instead I will touch upon three concepts which are peculiarly important to Teilhard's overall vision: complexity, love, Omega Point.

Evolution occurs through increasing complexity of organisms and systems. Complexity in time breeds consciousness. There is thus this extraordinary bind which could be called complexity/consciousness. The role of complexity in the unfolding of the evolutionary panorama is most remarkable. On one level, it is a mere description of the degree of organization of matter; on another level (that of consciousness and self-consciousness) it is a creative principle of the transformation of less knowing systems into ever more knowing intelligent systems.

The epistemological import of the idea of complexity has been neither fully grasped nor explored. If complexity holds the key to the transformation of all living processes, then it means that *the epistemology of evolution must be rooted in our understanding of the nature of complexity.* Let us reflect how remarkable it is that through

46

mere increase of complexity we obtain *new knowing systems*. Complexity is, then, this process which makes the actual out of the potential. More than that: it even creates the potential. The more complex the system, the more performance it is capable of and therefore the more potential it contains. If so, then complexity emerges as a critical concept of evolution—the hidden spring which guides the intricacy of our process of understanding.

But there is a problem here. For it would appear that "the more advanced, the more complex." Yet, when we look at the products of human culture, something different emerges. The greatest works of art are so *simple*. Also on the level of spiritual attainments of the human being, love, grace, and compassion are so simple. And, finally—Omega Point. In spite of its staggering complexity, it *must* be simplicity incarnate. Perhaps our language breaks down on this level of discourse. Perhaps the relationship between the simple and the complex is more *complex* than our language can convey. Perhaps the simplicity of this relationship will reveal itself when *we* become more complex, in that sense, that is, in which Lyall Watson talks about the brain: "If our brain were so simple that we could understand it, *we* would be so simple that we couldn't."

In our symbolic creations, we convey much through little; above all we express *essence*, which shines through the material substance. Perhaps the explanation of the dilemma is that in metamorphosing itself into spirit, matter goes through an incredible trauma of complexity to become suddenly simple—in the symbolic manifestations of beauty, grace, and holiness. This is how I see the phenomenon of Aphrodite of Knidos. The geological process that ended up in the creation of marble was very complex. The creative process of the sculptor making the statue was very complex as well. But the symbolic meaning of the final product is staggeringly simple. There is a dilemma here, a fascinating puzzle of evolution, namely that at times its increasing complexity resolves itself in patterns of exquisite simplicity.

Another dilemma which Teilhard poses for us all is his

conception of love. He claims that love is *the affinity of being with being*, and, as such, it is not peculiar to man. "It is a universal property of all forms of life and thus embraces all forms of organized matter. . . . Recognizing the presence of it in ourselves we must (as we did with consciousness) *presume its presence in everything that is*" (*The Phenomenon of Man*, p. 290).

This conception I do not find helpful. Indeed, I find it misguided. For it takes away *uniqueness* from the phenomenon of love. If love is spread out through all forms of organized matter, then there is nothing unique about it in human beings. I am, on this issue, in agreement with Arnold Toynbee, who insists that "love and consciousness are products of evolution, of the stage at which evolution has generated the human social animal."

If we assume that both consciousness and love are latent attributes of all matter, then we might just as well assume that *everything* that ever emerges in evolution is somehow already stored there. But if we assume that, we make of evolution a rather *trivial* process—the agent which only unveils what is already there. We also make ourselves vulnerable to the argument that evolution is at the mercy of the Divine Plan, of the pre-established harmony, or simply God's design. We then remove from evolution its creative power.

But evolution is creative through and through. The concept of emergence in evolution is of key importance. Evolution did not proceed according to any pre-established course. While creating some options, it discarded other options, just as it happens in human life. The emergent qualities of evolution are simply those which *emerged* as the result of contingent developments in evolution, and not because they were programmed in the evolutionary process. If the latter were the case, then we should not talk about emergent evolution but of a preprogrammed one. So we have to decide: either evolution is creative and emergent, therefore indeterministic, or it is entirely programmed and therefore determined from the start. In my view, it is only by accepting the former alternative that

48

we can make sense of evolution in human terms; that we can talk about responsibility within the evolutionary framework; that we can talk about our will and freedom while contributing to the creative process of evolution. If we were to accept the latter alternative, we would all be reduced to preprogrammed puppets.

The third dilemma which I wish to discuss is concerned with Omega Point vis-a-vis Christianity. Let met start with this dilemma straight away. There is a profound inconsistency in Teilhard's view of evolution. On the one hand, it is for him a *forward* unfolding process which culminates at Omega Point, at the end of time; and on the other hand, it is a process of going *back* to the original Christian God.

By attempting to subsume Omega Point under Christian theology, Teilhard undermines the *raison d'être* of evolution as an unfolding and self-actualizing process. For if evolution is a return to Christ, a return to the original Paradise, then it only recapitulates the past. If, on the other hand, evolution is actualizing itself, and will be only actualized at the end of time, then there is no return to Paradise Lost, for *there never was a Paradise*. There was only a brutish, incoherent beginning. Little literary metaphors such as the story of civilization beginning in a garden and ending in a city (Eden and the New Jerusalem) are of little help. These stories are profoundly influenced by the language and framework of the Judeo-Christian tradition, based on the notion of Paradise Lost to be regained. The Omega hypothesis of evolution maintains, on the other hand, that we never return, for evolution is an arrow made of barbed wire.

Let me elaborate this dilemma a bit, as it is of great importance. If we recognize the notion and the authority of God as conceived in the traditional religions, particularly Christianity, then our evolution, including the moral and spiritual one, is completed. What we *can* do, and the only thing we can do, is to *return* to the Paradise Lost, to re-acquire virtues that have been bestowed on us by God-the-Original-Maker. If, on the other hand, we see ourselves as unfinished spiritual beings, indeed only in the infancy of our evolution, then we simply cannot accept the traditional notion that God made us perfect. Our alleged perfection makes nonsense of our actual imperfections. When we contemplate our primordial beginnings in the cosmic dust, they appear far from godly. Our actual imperfections can then be well understood, as well as our striving for perfection. We become godly only at the end of our road, not at the beginning. And only if we actualize God in ourselves. For God is in the making— within us. God is spirituality actualizing itself in us. The idea of God within makes perfect sense. The further we go in our evolutionary journey, the closer we may approach him. Our journey is therefore to transcend— further and further, and never to return, for a return represents a fall from grace. Thus evolution resolves the intractable dilemma of traditional religions: how to explain man's imperfections while at the same time claiming that he is a divine being.

There is a way of incorporating the Christo/Genesis into the evolutionary design, namely by treating Jesus, not as God, a point of final destiny and of ultimate strivings, but as a symbol, an inspiration, a reminder that even at this early stage of our evolutionary journey we are capable of so much grace and divinity. Then Christ-consciousness becomes, not so much the ritualistic identification with Christ's body or blood, but more of an imaginary flame that illumines our roads towards greater grace and consciousness, a constant reminder of what our destiny should be and where we are going.

Paolo Soleri (b. 1919), perhaps the most creative follower of Teilhard's vision, crystallized its essence into concrete and stone. He asked himself: If we think about evolution *after* self-consciousness and culture have emerged, what are the main instruments of this evolution? Civilizations. If we think about civilizations as promoters of evolution, what are the main vehicles of civilization? Cities.

If we think about cities as main vehicles of civilizations, what are the aspects of cities that are most important for their function? The accumulation and integration of arts and crafts, of learning and doing, of creeds and occupations, of logistics and social institutions.

If we think about present cities as failing in this, their most significant function, what are the main causes of their decay? Disintegration and disassociation; excessive specialization and ruthless polarization; estrangement of social institutions from human concerns; divorcement of the entire ethos of cities from the overall direction of evolution.

If we think about possible ways of healing existing cities—making them again into instruments for enhancing civilization and for the growth of human consciousness and man's spirituality—what are the possible remedies? The reintegration of cities into radiant organisms: remaking them into the image of man.

It is at this point that Soleri and his idea of Arcology become relevant. Arcology represents the fusion of architecture and ecology. It is ecological architecture in our era of ecological crisis. In a more specific sense, Arcology designates a new conception of the city, of the urban habitat that is integrated, radiant, well functioning, life supporting—made in the image of man. For arcologies are crucial, environmental shells for carrying on the business of civilization and therefore the process of augmenting man's consciousness.

Arcology is an expression of the unshakable conviction that our evolutionary destiny is in our hands. It proclaims that we are evolution conscious of itself, that evolution self-actualizing itself through us now calls for the creation of new conditions. To Soleri, these conditions should facilitate a further process of *miniaturization*, which is his term for the complexity/consciousness process in its continuous unfolding. Without a doubt, Soleri's venture is a most far-reaching attempt to translate Teilhard's vision into architectural, environmental, social, and aesthetic terms.

Let me now express some reservations. Soleri is so much taken with the *infinite* grace of Omega Point, with the *infinite* beauty and with the *ultimate* point of our journey (which, after all, are extrapolations of our present mind) that he tends to think that our present attainments (that is, the present attainments of evolution) are quite negligible. In his opinion, we have nothing yet to celebrate.

In my opinion we have a great deal to celebrate. We are already divine, though our divinity is still pale. *The immanent is part of the transcendent.* Whatever we may make of grace at the final stage of our journey, it is only the enlarging of grace we have known in our own experience. If we didn't know grace now, we could not conceive of infinite grace. By thinking so little of present acquisitions of evolution, Soleri diminishes the potential transforming value of grace and love. As Teilhard makes too much of love—seeing it embodied even in rocks —so Soleri makes too little of it.

The belittling of our present condition of grace and of divinity leads to some important existential consequences. If what we have is so little, if what an individual can contribute is still less if anything at all, then what sense does it make to talk about taking into our hands the responsibility for further evolution? Individual human destinies are felt to be of utter insignificance. This kind of philosophy enacted in Arcosanti, the first arcology under construction, (in central Arizona under the leadership of Soleri himself), makes the residents feel dejected and inwardly crushed: their contribution and indeed sacrifice seem to amount to so little.

The point is that we must never treat others as instruments. Individual human destinies are as important as the process of the building of Arcosanti. We must never sacrifice individuals for the sake of an idea; for if the idea is right it should enhance individuals, not suppress them.

Soleri is fond of saying "shell before performance," which means that one first builds the physical environment, the shell of a new city, and only then fuses it with spiritual content. The continuous insistence on the shell, on the building edifice, on the construction process has been so pronounced that some think of Arcosanti as a non-spiritual place; others see it as a disguised worship of technology implicitly promoting atheism. Those who have experienced Arcosanti in some depth know that it is a life-enhancing environment, and potentially a spiritual, place. However, *evolution never builds a shell first and fills it with content later.* "Morphology recapitulates Spirit," says Teilhard.

The creation of right environments must go hand in hand with the creation of right people, of people with right minds, right sensitivities. The immanent is a part of the transcendent. The reconstruction of our inner self is part and parcel of the reconstruction of the larger environment of which we are an intrinsic part. Soleri seems to believe passionately that we cannot directly will to be different from what we are, but we can choose what we shall be now by choosing the environment that will mold us. Yet it is equally true that we cannot hope to create a new environment, indeed a new reality around us, which will mold us favorably, unless and until we sufficiently shape ourselves inwardly to allow the environment to have a positive influence on us. Beautiful environments received by ugly minds will make no difference to human destinies. Only those who are sensitive enough can receive the environment sensitively. 'Reality' out there is continually co-created by our sensitivities. Thus, no outside environment can do for us the work of our inner reconstruction.

Arcosanti is still *potentially* one of the places in which new radiance can emerge. But this new radiance will not emerge unless and until we admit *now* the divinity in man; unless we actively acknowledge reverence for life; unless spiritual quests are recognized and pursued as a part of our daily reality.

Man's eternal quest to find the right path whether through meditation or through the right environment, has no easy answer. Man in the East has pursued the path of meditation and has been overwhelmed by our technological prowess. We in the West have pursued the path of external reconstruction, and we have been overwhelmed by inner cancers and outer environmental plagues. Material progress is now a shell ringing hollow. With Teilhard we must find a structure suitable to the next stage of our evolutionary journey, which is a stage of our spiritual journey, one that will include not only a few select Brahmins but all mankind.

6
Rational Mysticism

"It is important to have a secret, a premonition of things unknown. . . . One must sense that he lives in a world which in some respects is mysterious; that things happen and can be experienced which remain inexplicable; that not everything which happens can be anticipated. The unexpected and the incredible belong in this world. Only then is life whole." (Carl Jung) We are the inheritors of a tremendous store of knowledge and of tremendous confusion. We have conquered the moon, conquered Everest, pushed the athlete's physical prowess to ever new limits. But we have never sorted out ourselves inwardly. And our moral codes are all in pieces.

We have inherited at least three moral codes, one grafted on the top of another. We have the Judeo/Greco/Christian tradition, the Renaissance tradition, and the positivist/scientific tradition. Each claims a part of each of us. Together they disintegrate us.

Reason and mysticism are unevenly distributed in these traditions. Since we are confused about our entire heritage, we are confused about the place of reason and of other faculties, including mysticism, in the plan of our being and living.

When we reflect on the relationship between reason and mysticism, we need to go back some 3,000 years to the time before the distinctly Western rational tradition started to crystallize around the Aegean Sea, before the

Greek genius and its particular brand of rationality started to mold our reason and our perception. Before that time the East and the West had not yet separated; mysticism was a form of reason and reason a form of mysticism. This is so in the *Upanishads*. And this is so at the dawn of the flowering of the Greek mind, with Pythagoras, Anaxagoras, and even Plato. Only with Aristotle did we start to chop, separate, and define.

Aristotle was the inventor of the rational, conceived as that which can be abstracted and separated from the rest and on which we can put a neat definitional label. Ever since his time we tend to think that if we can define things, then we know and understand them. But definitions can be lethal, that is, to the deeper sense of understanding. All-important knowledge is *contextual*. The context determines the meaning: the context of language, the context of culture, the context of life styles. Definitional meaning *separates* each word from the context of language and of culture and treats it as a separate and independent atom. It then makes molecular structures of atoms and insists or pretends that the life of culture and of spirit should conform to these artificial molecular structures.

Of the various definitions of mysticism, one given by the *Encyclopedia Britannica* strikes me as closer to the heart of the matter than most. It defines mysticism as: "the immediate experience of oneness with Ultimate Reality"; and it immediately adds that the mystical vision is ineffable, therefore cannot be put into words. We can agree that the phenomenon of mysticism is beyond definition. But there is more to language than definitions. Language not only describes and defines; it *conveys*. The power of conveying through language is sometimes rather miraculous. Through this power of conveying we can come close to the phenomenon of mysticism. Indeed, language itself may be the source of mysticism, as when poetry carries us so far and so deeply into the "other realm" that we become at one with all. Language is then the instrument of our mystical vision, or at least of our mystical experience.

An experience of reality is to a degree always the

experience of Ultimate Reality, for 'Ultimate Reality' is an aspect of 'ordinary reality,' and vice versa. There is one reality around us, not several of them. But it can be experienced differently, with various degrees of intensity, richness, and involvement—according to the power of our discrimination, perception, knowledge. Involvement and total absorption in it are prerequisites of the mystical experience of any reality. Detachment and cold objectivity (characteristic of the scientific attitude) are antithetical to the mystical experience; hence scientists, except those with the vision of an Einstein, make poor mystics; their detachment prevents them from entering this other realm of experience. Being totally submerged in the contemplation of a flower for a second or two is a rudimentary form of mystical experience.

We are all mystics—at least of low intensity. Any experience which in a very intense way transforms our being and affects our seeing can justly be called a mystical experience, for such an experience is invariably beyond our reason.

Every act of understanding is a natural mystery. Every time sparks fly through our mind and we grasp *it* and comprehend *it*, there is an act of grace. Let me put it in a paradoxical manner: it is quite *incomprehensible* that we comprehend anything. Whenever the mind is set in motion we always bridge darkness and light, the mysterious and the natural, the rational and the mystical.

The emergence of mind and the phenomenon of mind itself are among the ultimate mysteries of human existence and of the existence of the universe. That we know anything is a mystery. That we behold a splendid, radiant sun in us, the mind, which illumines and enables us to *see*, is a miracle if there ever was one for us to witness. The brain—lump of grey matter, pitifully small and awkward in its shape—when used by man becomes light that makes all else alight and alive.

Mysticism is a phenomenon much larger than its religious embodiment. Now the question is: If we divorce mysticism from traditional religion, and particularly from the notion of traditional deity, will we not impoverish the whole context of the mystical experience and the whole phenomenon of religion? Not necessarily so. How do we make sense, then, of Jesus and the Buddha? Jesus and the Buddha are the first approximations to God, first sketches of God-in-the-making. Jesus and the Buddha are the demonstrations of the *possibility* of God, not the statements of his actuality and *finality*. We understand the meaning of Christ and the significance of the Buddha— we understand the sense in which they are symbols of God—but only insofar as there is a spark of godliness in ourselves, only insofar as we have become, even in a dim way, sparks of divinity ourselves. Trees and rocks are unlikely to share our notion of divinity, for they are in more rudimentary stages of matter becoming spirit.

So far, we have seen God but in very fragmentary manifestations, because only fragments of God have emerged through evolution and through us. Jesus and the Buddha are two shining fragments. They are continuous reminders of the possibility and a continuous challenge to our destiny, which is also the destiny of God-in-the-making. Rational mysticism maintains:

> that mystery in the world is as natural as the falling of leaves in the autumn;
>
> that there are things which are beyond our knowledge, not only because they have not yet been penetrated by science, but because mystery is in the nature of the world we dwell in;
>
> that the ineffable and the transcendent are part of our world and give meaning to our lives; or at least significantly contribute to the meaning of life;
>
> that the communion with the whole human family and of all beings is as rational as it is indispensible. A mystical bond with all other beings is a precondition of our sense of belonging, without which we remain aimless and lost;

that within the scope of our mind we possess faculties that go beyond the narrowly rational and enable us to grasp aspects of knowledge which are seemingly transrational: being peculiar to human rationality is a faculty of self-transcendence;

that the appearance of the mind is one of the lasting mysteries. When we go from mind to reality and from reality to mind we travel a passage of mystery;

that rationality and mysticism are aspects of the larger spectrum of knowledge starting from the amoeba and reaching Point Omega;

that poetry continually transcends the reality it describes and is therefore an expression of rational mysticism.

7
Faith

Some think that faith is spurious, that it belongs to a
primitive stage of man's existence and is unworthy of an
enlightened man. Mistaken. Faith is essential to our
well-being. Faith is a necessary condition of our ontological existence. On the human level, the fabric of our
social and moral ideals, the fabric of culture and symbols,
is vast and elaborate. We can maintain this vast symbolic
substratum and in turn it can maintain us if we believe in the
sense and meaningfulness of the universe around us.
Faith is thus the cornerstone of meaning, a precondition of
our life.

In the phenomenon of faith we find an expression of
rational mysticism. We continually shape our life
through man-made symbols. But what are symbols? How
do they influence our life? There is a bit of mystery here.
Just imagine something nonphysical—be it the search
for the Holy Grail or the desire to become a *perfect* pianist—
that guides our life in such a way that we totally submit
to it. Those higher aspirations, represented by symbols,
pull us up from above. This pull is transrational, almost
mystical. There is no human life which has not experienced
these pulls from above.

We endow our symbols with meaning, and these
symbols, in turn, guide our lives. The whole process is
based on faith: faith in our symbolic codes, and faith in
the meaning of our lives as related to and expressed

through these transpersonal symbols. Those who lack faith not only undermine the meaningfulness of their lives; not infrequently when one's faith collapses, one's life collapses, so fundamental is faith to the structure of our lives.

At present we are all surrounded by the cloud of an overwhelming confusion. Nothing seems to make sense, nothing seems to be promising, practical, worthy of undertaking. And yet, it is at such times that we must be able to lift up our gaze beyond the cloud of confusion to more distant horizons.

We may *have* to project ourselves into the future in order to see through the present confusion, in order to perceive that what we now consider necessary and inevitable is only contingent and tenuous. By projecting ourselves into the future we acquire clarity with respect to the present. This clarity is part of our liberation. Nothing is more crippling than the belief that what *is* must be.

Human life is inherently teleological. The teleological component of human life means that life is not only directed but also transcendent: we continually overcome ourselves, and the limitations of the world, striving towards higher and higher goals. In short, human life means transcendence, means projecting into the future. Thus, projecting into the future is a component of the meaning of human life.

The belief in the future is not an escapism from the present but a necessity of the human condition. It has always been a part of the human condition. For the future is constantly in the making. In order to mold the future, we have to believe that we have the power of molding. Any renovation must start with the renovation of confidence.

The flame of human life burns with the intensity of our wills and visions. We can transform our condition, and we *will* transform our condition. But only with the provision that there is a sufficient number of us endowed with strong wills and clear visions. The history of past failures, half-blind gropings, and mistaken beginnings is *not* evidence of the impossibility of the transformation. The history of evolution itself is the story of blunders.

61

Until and unless a new mutation has worked itself out, until a new transformation is accomplished, there is every reason to believe that this transformation is not possible. Just *before* we succeed with a new thing, our record is the history of blunders and the evidence of failures. Past failures are a bad criterion of our future potentials; we cannot derive the confidence in our belief in the more radiant future from bloody events of our past history.

We can derive confidence and must derive it from contemplation of the essence of our inner being, from our ability to conceive the future in the image of a transcendent man. We would not be able to imagine this other future if it were not a part of our essence. Imagining it, we extend ourselves and realize ourselves; we actualize the potential that is latent in our existence. This ability to envisage a transcendent future is not limited to some chosen individuals, but is given to us all. For we are all evolving beings. Each is gazing, if only indirectly, at the stars.

The prophets of darkness who now dominate the scene, and the legions of faceless, confused people who unwittingly support them, are not the ones who will pave the way to an alternative future. The human future is a set of fantastic variations played by the musician called Cosmos, is an imaginative drama which Cosmos plays with the possibilities. Cosmos is the player, we are the instruments. But not just passive instruments. We are co-players with the Cosmos. Once we have gained consciousness and self-consciousness, once we have become aware what a bloody and splendid drama the evolution of life has been, we are of necessity the co-players.

To be a player of the Cosmos, to be *anything*, we must have faith, which is the foundation of all meaning in human life.

To live in faith is to live in grace.

8
Intuition

Intuition is a form of knowledge. Intellect is a form of knowledge. Revelation is a form of knowledge. Mysticism is a form of knowledge. They are all parts of the kaleidoscope of matter becoming spirit. They are all aspects of evolution unfolding itself and seeking new forms of expression, which will be called perceptions, sensitivities, or categories of understanding, through which evolution will articulate itself further.

To the discursive mind, intuition is mysterious. To our intuition itself, intuition is not at all mysterious. Deep down we *know* that intuition is not only legitimate but also indispensible. We cannot support or justify this deeply embedded knowledge through logical reason, for this knowledge is *prior* to logical reason. In the final analysis it is intuition that redeems reason: all axioms of logic, geometry, and mathematics are accepted on intuition.

What is intuition from an evolutionary point of view? It is the living memory of the organism, indeed of the species. Intuition is the composer that orchestrates the organism's perceptions and conceptions, that coordinates both memories and perceptions in one huge cybernetic system. This system reacts to the environment unceasingly, almost automatically, and by and large correctly. It *must* react correctly, otherwise we would perish. Although it acts automatically, its complexity is simply staggering. Intuition—the grand coordinating agency—takes upon itself the work of sorting out and simplifying, and thus of making things manageable. Without it we would be lost in the endless stream of unorganized consciousness. If we were to use reason for every occasion of our life, we would have ended as the Bouridan's ass, always reasoning and never knowing what to do.

In its evolutionary ascent, the organism had to learn to play the cybernetic game: acting and reacting, receiving feedback and adjusting itself to complex situations— with cunning, accuracy and speed. *The sum total of this evolutionary cybernetic game we call intuition.* More precisely, intuition is a sum total of biological knowledge learned by the organism during its evolutionary ascent through the feedback process (often trial and error), which is well integrated with the organism's sensitivities and ready for instant use. Many so-called intuitive reactions appear *automatic*. But there is nothing automatic in the human organism—all is marvelously orchestrated. Intuition is the process of triggering off appropriate layers of memory and appropriate adaptive mechanisms to situations to which the organism has been responding for aeons of time. Let us remember that there was a time when there was no self-consciousness, no discursive, let alone logical mind which could manage our strategies for survival. So these strategies were stored in the body. They were stored in the eye. Intuition so often is the re-activation of the memory of the eye—the eye of the species, that is. The body was at the time the store and repository of our biological knowledge. It still is.

Intuition, in brief, is the faculty for managing the vast resources of the subterranean biological knowledge stored in us. These resources may be obscure to the discursive mind, but they are not unknown to our inner selves. Yet the logical mind seems to be often denying the validity of intuition as a form of knowledge. Yes, the logical mind of *some* who do not have the courage to go into their deeper layers and acknowledge the totality of their being.

Though important as intuition is we shall not deny the

64

use and greatness of rationality and logical reason. They too represent beautiful and *cunning* attainments of evolution. It is quite cunning to have an argumentative mind which can rationalize almost everything. Reason, logic, and language represent articulated forms of our intuition. Arguments are abstract linguistic responses to complex human situations. On their power and ingenuity our survival, in this cognitive world, so often depends. It was a great leap in our human evolution when, instead of splitting his head, we started to insult the opponent with words. Thus, logic and language are cybernetic (linguistic) responses of the organism to complex social situations. There is a close parallelism between instant and effortless responses of our body and instant and effortless linguistic responses of our mind; each is a part of the same cybernetic loop which we call life.

All things in nature have a tendency to transcend themselves. And so it is with rationality. Rationality and reason do not stay put and confined; they evolve, and change their scope and boundaries. Only the computer must stay within the limits of its programming. Human rationality always goes beyond itself, that is, beyond its fixed parameters, because it always functions within the larger context of evolutionary knowledge. The boundaries of the logical mind may at times be limited. But the logical mind is only a part of our larger mind. (See Mind I, Mind II, Mind III, Chapter 25.)

The discursive mind is the linguistic mind. The discursive mind assumes that words mean exactly what our cognitive theories of meaning intend them to mean. Human meaning, on the other hand, invariably contains not only the cognitive but at the same time the biological, the aesthetic, the social, the moral. Do not listen to those who maintain that words are atoms of which simple molecular structures must be made. Language is like a river, flowing through history; flowing through the lands of beauty and sublimity and embracing the grandeur of the stars; flowing through our murky, lower depths which influence and modify its meanings. Language is a mirror of the evolutionary drama. Strange as it may sound, *we are always saying more than we are actually saying.* This may be a paradox, but basically it is a homage that language pays to the exquisite complexity of human meaning—as embedded in biological knowledge, and as embedded in the entire evolutionary endowment. Words can say more (and they usually do) than linguistic theories can handle, for linguistic theories are abstractions of the discursive mind, while language expresses life, intuition, the whole evolution.

Glory to intuition which can grasp more than we can explain. Rely on intuition, evolution's enormous gift. But don't assume that intuition is infallible. Nothing is. Even computers make mistakes—and how often! Intuition is our pipeline to the subterranean region and also to the stars, to the world of mystery and to the world of fullness.

9
The Natural and the Supernatural

The natural and the supernatural are one. In unfolding
ourselves (and evolution in us) we transform the natural
into the supernatural. They are both parts of the same
vast spectrum. This spectrum is evolution devouring itself
—in the act of self-consummation, which is also self-
transcendence. By acquiring new sensitivities, that is, new
powers of experiencing and receiving, we make the
supernatural natural. We lift ourselves to the level of the
transnormal, which then becomes normal. Miracles are
the results of the powers and capacities which we have not
yet acquired.

I do not have the seeing eye. I have the thinking eye.
My retina is wired with all kinds of theories, including
scientific theories. Whenever I open my eyes and am guided
by them, I am guided—in a no less sophisticated manner
than transcontinental missiles guided by computers—
by an extraordinary network of theories and feedbacks.
When my eyes guide me, my knowledge and experience
guide me; the knowledge of the species guides me; the
knowledge of evolution guides me. My eye may not
know how much knowledge it possesses, but I do; it may
not be aware of the variety of sophisticated feedback
loops it contains, but I am. When I am guided by my seeing,
what does the guiding—my eyes, my mind, or my entire
being?

The sharp separation of thinking and feeling is spurious

and detrimental to our well-being. My thinking mind is also the feeling mind. My feeling body is also the thinking body. Yes, I think through my heart and feel through my mind. In my heart and in my mind I have stored the awareness of Plato and of St. Augustine, of Leonardo and Pascal, of Blake and Goethe, of Schweitzer and Teilhard. I have got them all stored in the layers of my being. I can see through their eyes because they have shaped my sensitivities, and these sensitivities are the filters of my mind.

According to the Romantics, the greatest achievements of the human spirit and therefore of the human race are of the heart and not of the mind. This is sham. The heart unaided by the mind is a sluggish, sloppy, sentimental fool. This must be said clearly because there is so much sentimentality in the air.

The most exquisite poems, the most compassionate forms of government, the most luminous forms of understanding, the most towering expressions of love, in brief, the greatest achievements of culture and of human spirit, came about not through the explosion of feelings, but through the explosion of *mind*.

Feelings resolve nothing. Unenlightened feelings are like Furies. The Greeks were judicious enough to personify uncontrolled feelings as destructive furies. When Furies descend upon Greek heroes, this is the beginning of the end; it leads to calamity and tragedy. Pure feelings resolve nothing. But enlightened feelings, as filtered through reason, are the beginning of wisdom.

The great mystic of all times, Jesus Christ, was at the same time a supreme embodiment of reason. He had the power of *seeing* and the power of *saying*. We do not quite see what he saw, yet through his power of words it is somehow revealed to us; it is partly revealed through the active participation of our mind, which is not alien to mystery as mystery is a part of its natural habitat.

From Pythagoras and Anaxagoras the Western mind —at its best at least—has continually blended the mystical

68

and the rational in its products and activities. To pick up only the rationalist/scientific tradition from Western culture is to pick up only part of that culture, and not the best part.

Pythagoras the mystic is as much alive in the memory of our culture as is Democritus the atomist. Anaxagoras's conception of *nous* (reason, mind) as all-pervading was the foundation of Plato's philosophy, which is the foundation of a major part of Western thought. Plato and Sophocles and Phidias in antiquity; St. Augustine and Thomas Aquinas in the Middle Ages; Leonardo da Vinci and Michelangelo during the Renaissance; Pascal and Spinoza, Goethe and Blake, Nietzsche and Rilke in modern times; Schweitzer and Teilhard de Chardin in the 20th century—all are a monumental testimony of the shining qualities of mind that reveals and illuminates, of mind that is part of the divine, of mind that is both rational and mystical. The abstract logical mind, which often goes under the name of scientific rationality, is a confined mind. The confined mind must not be the measure for the total, all-embracing mind.

If you think that your mind is an abstract, programmed machine separated from the rest of your being, then (with some effort) you will make your life in the image of the machine. If you think of your mind as exquisitely woven in the rest of your being, which is woven in the tapestry of creation, then, by acting on your belief, you may partake in the magic of creation. Reason is both the incarnation of the mechanistic and of the transcendental whose other name is the creative, the divine.

Let us therefore treat reason as a benevolent god in us, for godly attributes it certainly possesses. It is reason that makes the supernatural natural and that makes the natural divine. The people of the Enlightenment were right in worshipping reason. They were wrong in confining reason to a rather trivial scope. Glory to the evolutionary mind, for it is our light, the unifier of our experience, the ladder which helps us to reach higher steps of our being.

10
Sri Aurobindo
and Auroville

Among the 20th century intellectual and spiritual leaders of India, the three towering ones were Gandhi, Tagore, and Sri Aurobindo.

Sri Aurobindo's view of evolution as perfecting itself through the human species is so close, at times, to that of Teilhard that one simply is astonished. The two men never met. Neither heard of the other's theory at the time he was creating his own. How, then, can there be so much similarity?

The key to the secret is, in my opinion, the French philosopher Henri Bergson. The young Aurobindo was educated in Britain at a public school and then at King's College, Cambridge, at the turn of the century, when Bergson's philosophy was not only known but influential. Bergson's influence on Aurobindo was profound and yet it is totally concealed, as it was creatively transformed within the Hindu tradition. Others who have studied both Aurobindo and Bergson have confirmed my conjecture of the profound but concealed influence of Bergson on Aurobindo.

The idea of the *Zeitgeist* is not a fiction after all. Perhaps at a certain stage of its own articulation, evolution was bound to create two systems articulating itself in a very similar manner. But the similarities between Teilhard and Aurobindo should not be exaggerated. For Aurobindo's is essentially an Eastern system which belongs to the tradition of the *Upanishads*. It also places a great deal of importance on the practice of yoga; yet the system is formulated in accordance with Western intellectual standards. Traditional Indian scholars have often been chagrined by the liberty Aurobindo took in reinterpreting Hindu doctrines in a novel and radical way; however, they seem to have forgiven him because he was so illuminating in interpreting the *Upanishads*.

The continuous leitmotif of the *Life Divine* is the most striking feature of Aurobindo's system. This is also the title of one of his books which celebrates divinity in life in a most fervent, sweeping, and eloquent manner by relating it compellingly to the entire tapestry of human life—including individual destiny, social destiny, and cosmic destiny of human beings. We are struck that his idiom and argument are totally Western: "Man occupies the crest of the evolutionary wave. With him occurs the passage from an unconscious to a conscious evolution" (*The Life Divine*, 1918, II, 23). "An evolution of consciousness is the central motive of terrestial existence. The evolutionary working of nature has a double process: an evolution of forms, and evolution of the soul." "A change of consciousness is the major fact of the next evolutionary transformation, and the consciousness itself, by its own mutation, will impose and effect any necessary mutation of the body" (*The Life Divine*, 1918, II, 23).

"*Life evolves out of Matter, Mind out of Life, because they are already involved there: Matter is a form of veiled Life, Life a form of veiled Mind. May not Mind be a form and veil of a higher power, the Spirit, which would be supramental in its nature? Man's highest aspiration would then only indicate the gradual unveiling of the Spirit within, the preparation of a higher life upon earth*" (*The Future Evolution of Man*, p. 25).

Can there be anything closer to Teilhard in content and style? Yet, at the same time, the system is steeped in the magma of the Hindu mythology. As such it requires the acceptance of numerous assumptions specific to Hindu religion and a whole range of concepts specific to Indian philosophy.

Aurobindo's striving for the Life Divine is so relentless that in the process, the human condition, and particularly the social condition, are somehow left in obscurity and neglected. The urgency of transcendence is so overwhelming that the immanent importance of grace and love is somewhat lost.

Another fundamental dilemma arises when we examine the way evolution actualizes itself through us. Although the transformation of consciousness is an enormous task, it is envisaged by Aurobindo as if it could happen almost tomorrow. The Divine Utopia is almost at hand—if only we practice our individual yoga diligently. This has an enormous appeal to individual psychology: *we* can save the world *now*. The ease with which Aurobindo promises salvation makes one wonder. Yet the creation of the system of integral yoga (see *The Synthesis of Yoga*), which provides steps for the individual mind in its journey of transcendence, is a towering achievement. Western thinkers are very weak in providing the techniques for the soul. Here Aurobindo is a master.

On the other hand, there is a peculiar problem with Aurobindo's thought. He claims that evolution is perfecting itself and so goes from *less* perfect stages to *more* perfect ones. However, the final stage of divinity is a *return* to the Atman, the Absolute, the One. Those two notions—eternal Brahman on the one hand, and unfolding and self-perfecting evolution on the other—are incompatible. The emergent qualities of evolution must not be reduced to the attributes of traditional deities. Within a truly *evolutionary* perspective we must see the increasing perfection that we acquire as ultimately going beyond anything accomplished in the past, and to a degree that is unimaginable even in the great religious systems of the past.

Teilhard and Aurobindo are among the foremost rhapsodists of the glory and greatness of evolution. The ultimate inconsistency of their views on evolution lies in their divided loyalty: to the inexorable, creative and transforming power of evolution on the one hand, and to traditional perfect, finished God on the other.

The story of Aurobindo does not end with Aurobindo himself. The continuation of this story is in the Mother and Auroville. What is Auroville? An intentional community of spiritual aspirations situated near Pondicherry in Southern India (100 miles south of Madras) where some 600 young people from some 50 nations are attempting to remake their lives in a more spiritual mold. They are also attempting to lay new foundations (by personal example) of a new international co-operation and a new international world order.

The influence of the Mother is all-important. Without her there would be no Auroville. Who was the Mother? She was born Mira Alfassa in Paris on February 21, 1878. An accomplished painter and musician, she began to have psychic and spiritual experiences at a very early age. In 1914 she came to India, to Pondicherry, and at once recognized Sri Aurobindo as the teacher who allegedly had been guiding her spiritual development, in an occult way. After spending the period of the First World War in France and Japan, she returned to Pondicherry in 1920 and resumed her collaboration with Sri Aurobindo. The Mother has in fact made the ashram at Pondicherry known throughout the world. She conceived the idea of Auroville. She gave it the impetus. She designed it and helped to lay the foundations. Under her guidance, in 1968 the urn containing earth from 121 countries was laid. She died in 1973. But her influence on Auroville and its inhabitants is enormously important. She keeps them all in her spiritual grip.

Aurobindo preached the doctrine of divine anarchy; he probably got it from Pitrim Sorokin, a sociologist-philosopher, born in Russia, who preached anarchy as an alternative social system. When asked about the future political system of Auroville, the Mother replied, echoing Aurobindo: it shall be divine anarchy. However, anarchy without being divine is a bit of a problem. This is what one experiences at Auroville. Still, whatever gripes one might have about present chaotic conditions, what stands out in one's memory are those resourceful individuals who are doing the real work. What holds them all together? Their high ideals, which give them strength, and the awareness that they are incomparably rich—in spite of the harsh physical conditions—in relation to the empty lives they would have led in the West.

Within Auroville there are many Aurovilles. There is Auroville as Great Adventure, for those for whom the West is burned out and unable to provide new and sustaining options. Most Aurovillians are those who are simply unable to live in the West, in that "terrible machine." There is the Escapist Auroville, in which many stray children of the hippy revolution found shelter, and in which they play with toys called "Future" while surrounded with flowers and trees. There is the Spartan Auroville in which a group of brave young people from the comfortable West are living under trying conditions, attempting to work out a new idiom of life in the coming age of scarcity. In their personal life they attempt to show how the global society, the West in particular, must change in order to survive and establish a new socioeconomic order.

There is the Ecological Auroville—and this one is of great importance—in which reclamation of the land washed out by erosion is taking place, whereby the land is forested and finally turned into blooming gardens. This Auroville is not only the pride and joy of all Aurovillians but a sober and salutary lesson to all humanity. A part of this Ecological Auroville is the Gatherer's Paradise: a piece of land of about 50 acres allowed to be returned to the primordial state of forest and bush, on which no agriculture is permitted, not even a plough or a cow, with not even bicycles allowed inside. People here live by the fruit of the earth, the berries and what the trees and the bushes yield—in a sense setting evolution backward. Yet one cannot help admiring their consistency and purity, their sense of purpose and of experiment.

There is the Spiritual Auroville in which particular individuals attempt to come to terms with their inner life and elevate it to a higher spiritual level. There is the Mystic

74

Auroville, said to be finished and ready, fully realized, as it were, in a Platonic heaven. As people of Auroville construct the physical Auroville, they only unfold what is already there—in the mystic reality. This last Auroville is not to be seen by the ordinary ignorant eye as it is in the other reality—only slowly actualizing itself in concreto.

The 'true' Auroville is somehow hidden in this peculiar blend of myth and reality. As with all great societies and cultures, it is emerging by people enacting a myth and transforming it into a reality. The psychological key to this transformation is given by Sri Aurobindo: "Adore and what you adore attempt to be."

11
Reverential Thinking

Emmanuel Kant has maintained that reason without action is impotent and action without reason is blind.

Action tied to a myopic reason brings about myopic results; action tied to one-dimensional and over-specialized reason brings about unprecedented alienation and ecological devastations. Our one-dimensional, over-specialized thinking has turned out to be thinking against nature and not with nature, against human culture and not with culture; against human happiness and not for human happiness.

We have perceived the limitations of our analytical, objective thinking for quite a while. As an antidote, all kinds of correctives have been devised. Among those correctives cybernetic thinking and systems thinking are most striking examples. When we look into the scope and magnitude of our present problems, however, we realize that those correctives are clearly insufficient. They are insufficient because, although they have overcome certain forms of one-sidedness, they remain themselves one-sided and over-specialized.

When we look at nature and nature's ways of "thinking" and of connecting things, we immediately realize that connectedness occurs on all levels of nature's being. Nature does not recognize the kind of boundaries that we have devised in our systems of knowledge, whereby we separate various phenomena in strictly separated boxes. Nor does nature recognize the distinction between the descriptive and the normative, between the objective and the subjective. Nature is ceaselessly normative in its modus operandi. The connectedness of nature cuts across categories and levels established in our descriptive sciences. It can be said without exaggeration that goodness, truth, and beauty are one and the same for nature, are aspects of each other.

If there is any clue to be taken from nature with regard to our thinking, it is this: our most creative and therefore most viable thinking in the long run moves freely across all levels of our knowledge and of our understanding. It is the kind of thinking that can connect the most unexpected elements and layers; the kind of thinking that is not imprisoned by, or regimented through, existing categories and existing disciplines. Indeed, this kind of thinking—connecting unexpected elements from different levels of knowledge—has produced the most striking human inventions and the most original breakthroughs in human knowledge.

The connected thinking which is required and, indeed, necessary for a viable global future of the human family will have to recognize itself as normative. One of the main deficiencies and, indeed, perils of our one-dimensional, over-specialized thinking (including cybernetic and systems thinking) has been the assumption that our thinking should be "clean," clinical, objective, neutral. In fact, it has never been that; it has always been at the service of some normative purposes, and always laden with values.

What I am suggesting is that we explicitly recognize the normative character of our thinking, particularly when it involves multiple relationships with ecological habitats, and especially with cultural habitats. Moreover, I suggest that we should go one step further and recognize what I should like to term *reverential thinking*.

Reverential thinking, when employed as a mode of our understanding on a large scale, will produce numerous and far-reaching consequences. It will affect and re-structure our perception. Our perception will no longer be a cold scanning of what material benefits we can derive from a given piece of the physical universe, but will become a celebration of life.

Reverential thinking will also influence our perception of other human beings and our perception of ourselves. Reverential thinking will affect our ideas about economics and about management. Ultimately, reverential thinking is good economics, for it will inform and guide us on how to take care of our entire well-being while preserving the integrity and viability of other beings, including large scale ecological habitats, without which our well-being (even economic well-being) cannot in the long run be secured. Reverential thinking, when spelled out in detail and applied to our global problems, is not only justifiable but makes good wholistic sense, for it is the kind of thinking that enables us to understand in depth the multitude of facets of our physical and transphysical universe and the multitude of aspects of our human, social, and spiritual existence.

Thinking reverentially is not only using our grey cells in a new way; it is also embarking on a new set of values. When American Indians thought and maintained that there is a spirit behind every tree, they did not mean to say that there is a ghost-like apparition roaming around the tree. This was their way of expressing their reverence for nature, of expressing the fact that, for them, all living things are of intrinsic value. This form of value and this form of reverence is acknowledged in the Orient in another way: there is a Buddha in every blade of grass.

To think reverentially is first of all to recognize human *life* as an intrinsic value; it is to recognize *love* as an essential and indispensible modality of human existence; it is to recognize *creative thinking* as an inherent part of human nature; it is to recognize *joy* as an integral part of our daily living; it is to recognize the *brotherhood of all beings* as the basis of our new epistemological paradigm. Reverential thinking is a vehicle for the restoration of intrinsic values, without which we cannot have a meaningful future of any sort.

78

Reverential thinking recognizes and cherishes Albert Schweitzer and his "reverence for life." Unless we are inspired by the ideal of reverence for life, and hold this ideal as one of our principal values, and make this ideal a part of our ontological structure, we cannot, in truth, think reverentially. For thinking reverentially must come from the core of our being.

Reverential thinking is not a luxury, but is a condition of our sanity and grace. Those who do not think reverentially —at times at least—simply impoverish their existence. Thinking as calculation is one thing; thinking objectively according to the requirements of science is another thing. Thinking reverentially when we behold the universe in its intimate aspects, and fuse it with our love, and feel unity with it is yet another thing.

There is a conflict between objective thinking and reverential thinking. Objective thinking recognizes no grace and no reverence for anything. Objective thinking creates indifferent observers, people who have little care and love for society and human beings; for care and love are excluded by objectivity. It is as simple as that. Reverential thinking creates participators in the compassionate world, people who do not atomize and objectivize but act in a unitary and caring way; their very perception is informed and inspired by compassion.

Right meditation contributes to healing the world. Reverential thinking is a form of healing.

12
Language as Transcendence

We use language for naming, as we did at the time when we invented the spade, the axe, the needle. But once society started to evolve, we immediately started to attach new meanings to the old primitive and original ones. So a spade is not *just* a spade; it came to symbolize things prosaic. The needle came to symbolize something else: to needle somebody. The symbolic power of language assumes an enormous importance.

This came about not only in relation to objects of everyday life. Flowers came to symbolize life, and indeed rather tender aspects of human life: love and flowers are inseparable. Thus we have in English a beautiful term: "deflowering," which stands for a multitude of delights. The ancient Greeks were perfectly aware of the great symbolic significance of the act of deflowering. So they endowed Aphrodite with a special attribute: every time she steps into the river her virginity is renewed, so that she can be deflowered again.

The symbolic function of language also means its transcendent function. Symbols metamorphose the reality which they symbolize. If you needle somebody, you don't need a steel needle; those psychic needles are far more ruthless and devastating. The world of the human psyche is the world of symbols, through which we express the various states of our being.

There are two senses to the meaning of the phrase

"language is a vehicle of transcendence." In the first sense "transcendence" refers to the symbolic function of language within the scope of human culture, whereby language metamorphoses physical reality into a transphysical one: from the needle to needling, from flowers to deflowering.

The second sense of "transcendence" refers to evolutionary transcendence of the human species within the scope of the entire evolving cosmos. Language is then a recapitulation of the evolving universe. It reflects all the present acquisitions and tensions, cognitive and otherwise, with the unresolved dilemmas and half formulated gropings. Language also presages what is becoming— a part of the process of articulating what is emerging but not yet here. It is exceedingly difficult to name things which are in flux, and particularly those which are becoming.

Evolution works through us. We are its custodians and guardians. We are endowed with certain propensities and potentials. Our task is to actualize this potential: our duty is to carry on the process of evolution towards the next stages of development. We are evoking the sensitivity of matter, or put in other words, articulating the spirituality potential in us and in the cosmos. As evolution works through us, we work through language. Both men and language are processes and parts of a larger unfolding phenomenon. In this scheme of things, language is not only a recorder mirroring the accumulated dust of history; not only an exquisite tool for dialectical reconciliation of incompatible ontological domains, but itself a force of transcendence. Language embodies and further articulates the emergent qualities and attributes of the transcendent world. Language is a part of the self-articulation of the world; a part of self-actualization of man's consciousness, which in turn is a part of the self-actualization of the cosmos at large. Expressed otherwise, language is a part of the actualization of man's spirituality, and this is a part of the larger process of self-actualization of the universe.

The tensions and failings of language are failings of

Being actualizing itself. These tensions, contradictions, and apparent walls simply indicate, at the time that we reach and experience them (sometimes in despair), that new junctions of emerging transcendence have been reached. These are the junctions at which spirit (new emergent qualities) is transcending itself through us, and thus through the contortions of language which is unable to convey and express that which has not yet arrived.

Therefore, we should rejoice in these tensions and apparent contradictions of language, for they redeem our existential striving by indicating that we are going beyond, that we are transcending. There is no wall of language but only receding transcendental horizons that so far have escaped our grasp. There is no despair over the prison of language but only an existential predicament of the human being doomed to perfectibility, thus constantly attempting to transcend himself, constantly grasping beyond. Language is a part of this process—of being in the act of perpetual unfolding. It reveals in a telling and sometimes painful way our continuous quest for perfectibility.

All of this is quite close to Heidegger's conception of language. He also saw in language an ontological reality. He wrote: "Language is not simply one tool which man possesses along with many others. It is language that makes possible our standing within openness to what is." However, Heidegger is lacking the transcendental dimension. The vector of evolution seems to be missing in his plan of being, which is curiously static.

Now, in this compelling spectacle of being unfolding through us and through other creatures, the powers of language, at this stage of the cognitive development of the cosmos, are of profound significance. Language is one of the vehicles of culture articulating the flux of human existence in permanent forms. But more importantly: It is an aspect of the cognitive development of the cosmos, it is an ontological modality through which the cosmos is articulating itself, and articulating us as a byproduct. The cognitive strivings of man on the evolutionary scale are inseparably linked with language, which carries within itself the glories and the agonies of the evolving universe.

Language is a part of the tapestry of evolution. It has been woven into evolution at a certain point of its development. It will disappear from this tapestry at another point of the unfolding evolution—with the proviso, which I am here assuming, that the universe has the propensity to further and further articulation of its spirituality. If such is the case, then in the future language will be discarded as a spurious trapping and we shall be communicating much more directly, from spirit to spirit.

In this post-linguistic and perhaps even post-cognitive state, the tensions of language are ultimately resolved because transcendence is achieved; the spirit of man is liberated; the agony of matter is redeemed; the dialectic is carried to its ultimate point of non-being becoming being. In the eternal silence we shall effortlessly articulate all meanings.

13
The Language of Being

What happens when I touch you with my words? It is like touching you with my hands. Nay, better. The hand may be cold or it may meet a cold response.

When I touch you, I drill a corridor to your heart. Better still—to your soul. The language of being is the language of souls. It takes one soul to initiate it, and it takes another soul to receive it.

The soul does not like shouting. So the language of being is the language of whispers. When my soul whispers and your soul hears, we are together, we are at one, the cacophony of human strife overcome.

My words are full of messages. Some are trivial. Those the soul ignores, as it is tuned to finer things. When I touch you and you reverberate, you do so through the inner core of your nobility, through the subtle aspects of your human condition.

Without knowing it, I address myself to the ineffable in you, to the transcendental mystery in which we are all enshrined. You best respond to my language of being when I touch the sacred in you; for there is a substratum of the sacred in each of us.

In the silence behind words our sacred sides mirror each other. The language of being is the language of the sacred reverberating in you and me whenever we have the courage of silence to listen to each other carefully.

The language of being is the language of silence, is

acting from our true nature, is bridging the space between
you and me, so that, in Rilke's words:

> Without knowing our true place
> We act our true nature
> Antennae feel antennae
> And the empty space is bridged.

We do not just communicate—we commune. We indwell
in each other; we indwell in the larger Presence of which we
are a part.

The language of being is the language of *emanation*.
You receive the other through the invisible energy which he
spreads around himself. Right energy of the other makes
you seek his presence, gives you joy and comfort in his
company. This is the way Socrates' presence manifested
itself. His company was joy because the language of
his being was clear and powerful. His language of being
made the souls of others sing.

The soul is the window of the universe. The soul can
see through the language of being. The universe is as the
soul sees it—through the language of being. Through
the physical eyes we see the surface of the universe.
Through the eyes of the soul we see its depth. It is only in
this depth, only when we uncondition ourselves, that we
can achieve the autonomy which allows us to act
responsibly.

The language of being is creating a space in which
others can breathe and rest, a space in which they are not
intimidated or threatened, a space that is calming, a
space which imparts peace within. The language of being
can be developed—by sensitivity-feedback: by discovering
which configurations of your inner structure produce
the desired space; and by attempting to emulate this state of
your inner self that envelops others in the right space.

Maria Callas once said: "To sing is an expression
of your being, a being which is becoming." The language
of being is akin to singing in this sense—it is a language of
becoming; becoming your true quintessential self;

85

becoming that contributes to the becoming of others; becoming that is a beam of love.

There is no other joy so true or warm in this world as that of finding a great soul responding to your own.
Goethe

14
Wholeness, Hippocrates, and Ancient Philosophy

"Rejoice at your life for the time is more advanced than you would think."

Rejoice at your inner powers for they are the makers of wholeness and holiness in you.

Rejoice at seeing the light of day for seeing is a pre-condition of truth and beauty.

Hippocrates was one of the sages of antiquity. Born in 460 B.C. on the Island of Kos, he died on the same island in 377 B.C. He was blessed with illustrious ancestors: he was the 18th descendant of the god of medicine Asclepius on the side of his father, and the 20th descendant of Heracles on the side of his mother. He lived in the most glorious period of Greek history when everything worthy of the human mind came to fruition. It was his historic mission to lay the foundations of scientific medicine. Yet we have to pause here, for the term "scientific" covers a multitude of sins nowadays (in addition to a multitude of virtues). Therefore it would be more apt to say that Hippocrates was the father of systematic medicine; and something else should not be denied to him—that he was the father of *holistic* medicine.

Scientific knowledge, in our sense, was but in its infancy in the 5th century B.C. Surprisingly, however, Hippocrates somehow avoided making statements which scientific medicine would consider "dreadful mistakes."

What saved him was philosophy, a right kind of philosophy, and there was plenty of it in his time. Hippocrates' pronouncements were often as philosophical as they were medical.

Yet we must not exaggerate. Hippocrates was a supreme and consummate practitioner of medicine, not just a philosopher. He spent twelve years visiting all the renowned medical centers of the world of his time. He pursued every line of empirical inquiry that was open to him. In his asclepion or school of medicine in Kos, some 6000 medical herbs were recognized and used. Knowledge of the organism and its reactions to herbs must have been gloriously explored.

The asclepion was a place of healing as well as a place for learning medicine, a combined medical academy and hospital, or a university hospital. But these terms of ours do violence to the original conception of the asclepion. While our medical centers are places of sterility which we want to leave as soon as possible, it was quite the opposite with the asclepia of ancient Greece. There were some 300 of them, the ones at Epidaurus and at Kos being the most famous. Situated in inspiring surroundings, sheltered by classical buildings and temples, an asclepion was a place where you wanted to stay, not to leave as soon as possible. The healing surrounding was one of its primary assets. You can still feel it, even after twenty-four centuries of destruction, when you find yourself at Epidaurus, at Delphi, or at the asclepion of Kos.

The physical quality of the environment of the asclepion, though immensely important, was only one aspect of it. Each asclepion was dedicated to the god Asclepius; each was adorned with various temples which were an integral part of the healing process. The spiritual aspects of healing were viewed as an inherent part of the tapestry of living.

Ancient wisdom lacked knowledge of detail. But it did not pervert the meaning of the whole for the sake of detail, as we have done in recent times. For the ancients, to restore meant to restore the whole, whereas we are still

obsessed with details and want to be wholistic via piece-
meal strategies. The diseased empiricist mind is still
ticking away in its clock-like discreteness of the Newtonian
paradigm, oblivious of the wholistic nature of all reality.
The main problem with our fractured existence and our
fractured health is not the unhealthy social and physical environment in which we live, but the clinical, fractured
environment of our mind, which instinctively and in-
tuitionally we recognize as pathological, but to which we
nevertheless succumb in our institutional and public
life. The coercion of our public life becomes the curse of
our individual existence.

Hippocrates was worshipped in his time and the aureole
of glory is still upon him, after centuries of spectacular
advances in scientific medicine. He was made an honorary
citizen of Athens after he contained the plague of 430 B.C.
So great was his esteem that after Alcibiades destroyed
Kos in 411 B.C., for its insubordination to the Athenian
Alliance, this general was instantly ordered by Athens to re-
build the city for the sake of Hippocrates and his son
Thessalus.

Later on the king of Persia, Artaxerxes, requested that
Hippocrates come to Persia to fight an epidemic raging
there; in return Artaxerxes offered any amount of gold to
Hippocrates. But the feeling among the Greeks toward
the Persians was still hot and hostile. Hippocrates replied thus: "Thank you, Artaxerxes, for the honor and
confidence placed in me. However, it is impossible for me
to help a declared foe of my country. Consequently, both
the gold and the disease are yours to keep."

Artaxerxes, furious at this reply, sent a message to
the people of Kos telling them to surrender Hippocrates. If
they refused, their entire polis would be so devastated
that it would be impossible afterwards to distinguish
between the inhabited areas and the surrounding deserts
and sea. To this message the inhabitants of Kos replied:
"Artaxerxes, the people of Kos will never do anything
unworthy which would offend their divine ancestors and
Hippocrates, who is the glory of this island. We shall not

hand him over to you, no matter if this decision were to entail the most terrible consequences. The gods will not abandon us." The Gods indeed were with the people of Kos. According to the story, Artaxerxes got apoplexy when he read this insulting reply and died instantly.

Among the precepts which Hippocrates advocated were:

> Nature is the cure of illness.
> Leave thy drugs in the chemist's pot
> If thou can't heal the patient with food.

These precepts are so simple that they sound naive. But this simplicity was born of deep reflection and of the study of the philosophy of the time. One of the great influences on Hippocrates was Heraclitus who lived from 544 to 484 B.C. The legacy of Heraclitean thought was still alive. The story has it that Heraclitus offered his papyri to the gods at the asclepion at Ephesus, and this is where Hippocrates went to study them. A philosopher offers his scrolls to the gods to be kept at an asclepion; a medical practitioner goes there to study them: this expresses a wonderful unity of things.

From Heraclitus, Hippocrates learned the fundamental lesson that *all wears out*, that "nothing in this world remains unchanged but for one moment only. Everything changes aspect. It dissolves, merges with other elements and displays a new aspect, different from the previous one. This last appearance is to remain for another moment, then it dissolves, but nothing is lost . . ." Thus all is in a flux of continuous transformation.

Heraclitus was not the only major influence. Equally profound was the impact of Pythagoras (580-490 B.C.). From Pythagoras, Hippocrates learned that health, as wholeness, means that the body and the soul must be examined together; that there are spiritual laws which human beings can ignore only at their own peril; that human will ensures and completes the harmony between body, mind, and soul; that complete human beings are those who have grasped the sense of this harmony and implemented it in their own lives; and this harmony means thinking correctly, and living correctly, according to the law. The ancient people appreciated the value of philosophy for their own life. Now, for Pythagoras, *harmony* was the key term. Harmony holds it all, or nothing is held.

I should mention at this point that the notion of harmony was known to Hippocrates before he went to study Pythagorean thought. The idea of harmony indeed pervaded all of Greek culture. Yet Hippocrates was immensely pleased and strengthened in his beliefs when he found that such an illustrious philosopher as Pythagoras was upholding notions similar to his own.

Yet another philosopher who made his mark on Hippocrates was Anaxagoras (500-428 B.C.) who represented the transition from Pythagoras to Socrates. This was the philosophical world in which Hippocrates lived. What a galaxy of minds to be surrounded with! Add to them Socrates who was Hippocrates' friend, and you will receive the picture of enlightenment unmatched by any period of Western history.

Hippocrates was a milestone in the history of Western medicine and of Western thought, not because he was an industrious observer who also managed to amass more medical knowledge than anyone else at the time, but *because he could see the wholeness of the human condition.* He clearly realized that philosophy is not an entertaining intellectual game but the foundations in which our well-being is embedded. By extending this insight ever so slightly, we might say that illness is the result of holding a wrong philosophy—which permits one to behave foolishly and disharmoniously, which does not help one to perceive the body and the mind as a whole. The right philosophy, on the other hand, must aid one in the quest for deeper meaning which is a constituent of our overall wholeness.

One of the specific triumphs of Hippocrates, of which we are usually unaware, was his ability to integrate the two divergent strands of Greek thought—the Heraclitean and the Pythagorean. The one insists that everything is in flux and transformation, and the other insists that there is a pre-established harmony. These two strands have never been properly integrated in Western thought since Plato. Our culture has become transfixed with *being* at the expense of understanding the deeper nature of *becoming*; Plato has overshadowed Heraclitus. Therein lies the source of one of our deepest conceptual and spiritual troubles. We are unable to live with the flux and with uncertainty; we demand clarity, which in turn requires separation and cutting things into distinct slices. Our analytical science has been an expression of this quest for clarity. Strange as it may sound, Newtonian physics is much closer to the Pythagorean view of the world than we usually credit it for. After all, at the threshold of the Newtonian era stands Galileo with his Pythagorean dream of reading the book of nature which is written in the language of mathematics.

Our minds are too fragmented to allow us to see that cosmology is relevant to our correct thinking and our good health. The tragedy of Western philosophy and of the Western mind since the Renaissance (perhaps since Aristotle) has been our inability to generate cosmologies which are life-enhancing and supportive of our daily struggles, including the care for our health and our wholeness. Eastern philosophies have never lost sight of those supreme tasks: hence their enduring strength.

One of the great tasks on the agenda of the meaningful future is to find a new form of integration for Heraclitus and Pythagoras. The supreme secret of life-evolving lies in our understanding that we are dealing not with a static harmony but Dynamic Harmony. If we recognize Dynamic Harmony, we then recognize that all things are in flux, in transformation, in the process of becoming. At the same time we recognize the permanency of some spiritual laws which give meaning to the flux.

The creation of a new cosmology that will accommodate the Heraclitean and the Pythagorean traditions and will fuse them together in a new understanding of the cosmos, is not only a precondition of our health but a precondition of the survival of the planet. It is also a precondition of our coherent understanding of the world which has become so fractured in modern times. In the 20th century Teilhard de Chardin towers above the horizon as the man who was able to combine Heraclitus and Pythagoras in a magnificent new synthesis. More recently, Ilya Prigogine has been inspired by the same quest.

Let us ask ourselves in the end: What is wholeness? The essential point about wholeness is that it is not a description of the state of things, but a description—rather an experience—of the state of *being*. We tend to think of wholeness as a property of an aggregate of things outside ourselves, while in fact it is a highly subjective concept describing individually and existentially the state of our own being. It is in this sense that Ravi Ravindra maintains:

> It is also good to remind ourselves that any real reconciliation of the demands of the spirit and those of the body is not a matter of general mental abstractions such as "science" and "religion." It is only in a unique particular in an individual's soul that any such reconciliation has any meaning. It is only in the concrete existential situation in which I simultaneously experience and intentionally embrace the different forces of the two realms of spirit and body or religion and science that I have a possibility of wholeness. Otherwise, one remains fragmented, thinking about or wishing for wholeness. (*The American Theosophist*, Special Issue: "Science and the Ancient Tradition," Fall 1982, p. 352.)

So, once again, what does it mean to be whole? It is to be on good terms with the cosmos; which means understanding and respecting the *laws*, as Pythagoras conceived of them. Or to put it in Plato's terms: "Health is a consummation of a love affair of the organs of the body." Wholeness works like a magnet: you must be whole to enable the other to become whole; your magnet of wholeness activates the potential for wholeness in the other.

Writing and reading poetry is good for one's wholeness. Finally, to be whole is to be encompassed by the sense of the divine in the divine cosmos. If all these "definitions" do not begin to convey what we feel and recognize on instinct as wholeness of our being, then we have to resort to silence. "From the springs of silence comes all understanding. All great truths were conceived and recovered in silence."

Rejoice at listening to silence for it is the begetter of enlightenment.

Rejoice at your inner powers for they are the makers of wholeness and holiness in you.

Rejoice at your large philosophies for they are the foundations of your well-being and a precondition of correct thinking, correct acting and good health.

Rejoice at the joy of existence for it is the hidden source of your well-being.

15
Culture and Nature

The number of theories of culture is bewildering. There are the *organic* theories, which insist on the unity of nature and culture. There are the *anti-nature* theories, which insist on the radical disjuncture between nature and culture. The anti-nature theories of culture are more characteristic of the West than of the East. The East, with its cyclical and organic conception of the cosmos, almost of necessity regards culture as organic.

Behind anti-nature theories of culture there is a *Faustian* conception of man "who only lives once" and therefore lives recklessly and who considers the reality of power as the only reality. There is, on the other hand, a *Franciscan* conception of man behind the organic theories of nature: man as a steward and a transcendental wanderer who toils for the greater glory of the immensely splendid cosmos.

"Organic culture" in the standard interpretation means that each culture, as an organism, grows out of some inconspicuous seed, comes to fruition, flowers magnificently, and then slowly decays, leaving its remnants as nourishment for succeeding cultures.

But culture can also be viewed as organic in a deeper sense, in a cosmic sense: its emergence was one of the acts of the cosmic drama. The cosmos gave birth to nature; nature gave birth to man; man gave birth to culture. Culture gave birth to a new man—the cultural man, a thinking, compassionate, sensitive being. In this chain of being, man is the link connecting nature and culture. Man is a product of each. However, he is also the creator of both. For 'nature,' as we know it, is a creation of man's mind—an exceedingly subtle and complex notion which includes cosmological, economic, aesthetic, and ethical components. The original natural man did not possess our concept of nature; probably did not possess any concept of nature at all; even and especially when he was one with nature. *Nature, as we think and speak of it, is a highly evolved cultural product.*

There are countless aspects of our lives which science neither perceives nor can explain but which often decide about the vibrance, vitality, and sanity of our lives. We have emerged out of organic forms: amorphous, irregular, fluid. What is our body if not a conglomerate of irregular surfaces and oval shapes? Starting with the womb in which we were conceived, and including all those wombs in which the evolution of our species has been taking place—our being has been determined by amorphous and irregular shapes, round and female. This is the original geometry of nature. But then, with the rise of civilization, a different kind of geometry was forced upon us: linear, angular, and straight. Our "civilized" life is happening among linear, angular, often rigidly deterministic shapes, which in a sense do violence to our primordial, amorphous ones. From amorphousness we have come, to amorphousness we long to return!

The amorphous forms of nature are a condition of sanity. Consider the purpose of trees. Why do we rest so well among the trees? Why is looking at a tree at a time of stress a solace and comfort? Because it brings us back to the amorphousness of the original geometry of nature. For culture we go to a concert hall or theatre; for a total rest we go to primordial forests or rugged mountains.

When we look at the trees and submerge ourselves in them, we experience a sense of unity with them; we return to the geometry by which we were created. In a sense we return to the womb. No psychoanalytical interpretations should be read into this statement. My description is a straightforward assertion of the fundamental unity between us and the rest of the organic world. Why do we rest so well and so totally among the trees? Because they help us to get rid of "artificial geometries" which are a burden to our biological system. The deepest rest is always in primitive conditions, where human geometry is absent and where natural geometry prevails. Looking at a tree is always a rest, a return to nature from which we have emerged.

Culture as a whole represents a specific ontological realm, the realm of spiritual energy which emanates from its objects, its symbolisms, its values, its myths. Culture is a repository of the spiritual energy of a society, a nation, or a group of people. So conceived, culture functions as the nourisher of myths; the upholder and codifier of values; the nexus for symbolic interactions; the store of tales and artifacts.

We are always impressed by the artifacts of a culture, for they are its most visible and most numerous manifestations. It requires some effort to go beyond artifacts and understand the symbolism and the values behind a given culture. It requires still more effort and imagination to reconstruct the myths that inspire and inform values of the culture and shape its destiny. At the ultimate level of the alchemy of culture, symbolism, values, and the spiritual energy of a culture merge with each other and are aspects of each other. When a culture is in a decaying state, this is reflected in its negative energy and its non-sustaining symbolisms and values. An important part of the symbolism of a culture is its language, which may be a very powerful sustaining force. But when a given culture is withering, its language loses vitality, does not emanate energy, is deadening—as is the case with present day language.

The viability and long-range survival of human civilization lie in its diversity. This diversity means the diversity of human cultures. Thus, traditional cultures must be preserved, if only for the sake of ensuring the health of the race in toto. We have a dilemma, however: namely, how to reconcile the requirements of economic equity and of social justice on the global scale with the requirements of cultural diversity, cultural uniqueness, and cultural integrity. My answer to this dilemma is that we must preserve the diversity of cultures, their uniqueness and their specificity, even at the expense of the economic equity.

In saying so, I do not wish to preach the gospel of economic imperialism, whereby we accept economic affluence for the West and a substandard level of living for the rest of the world. Economic equity and above all social justice must be our ideal to be pursued relentlessly. We must not presume, however, that material affluence can be achieved by all or that universal affluence would be such a good thing.

The myth of economic abundance for all is illusory. Such abundance is a specific product of Western technological culture; it is part of the Western ideological design of salvation through material saturation. We must re-examine myths of other cultures. We must look at the viability of traditional cultures vis-a-vis the inviability of the present technological culture. We must look at the subtle and deep fountains of spiritual energy which traditional cultures contain and preserve in various forms; we must also realize that these fountains are not nourished by technological culture and one homogeneous civilization. After we have reflected on the nature of culture and the necessity for diversity within the human species, we can cast our judgment as to whether the myth of the technological culture—the economic abundance for all and salvation through material saturation—is superior and more sustaining to the many potent myths of traditional cultures.

Nature and culture are both products of the same all-encompassing mind. When this mind becomes diseased a rift between the two appears. When the mind is healed again the two complement each other.

16
Of Minds and Pigeons

Twentieth century philosophy has mummified our understanding of the mind. Instead of exploring its creative and extraordinary aspects, it continually attempts to reduce the mind to the scope of activities characteristic of pigeons. If you use the pigeon methodology, you are bound to arrive at a pigeon-like understanding. When I say "20th century philosophy," I mainly mean empiricist-bound, analytically-oriented philosophy of the Anglo-Saxon persuasion that dominates our present universities and that has exerted a considerable influence on our thinking all over the globe in the second part of the 20th century. Let me try to trace the historical circumstances that led to the elevation of the pigeon methodology based on this philosophy as the tool of universal understanding.*

Karl Popper is right: the road to understanding of the philosophical scene often proceeds via understanding the background knowledge situation. But Popper exaggerates when he maintains that to understand the background knowledge is to understand the vicissitudes of science.

---

*This chapter is slightly different in tone; perhaps a bit denser in content. The reader will have the opportunity to experience the flavor of typical philosophical arguments as they are exchanged among philosophers. We need to comprehend well the topography of the mind of philosophers if we are to go beyond their limitations.

Now, there were already some serious problems with the scientific understanding of the world in the second half of the 19th century. With the discovery of non-Euclidean geometries, space in the Newtonian sense started to totter. Since the absoluteness of space is one of the basic assumptions of the Newtonian system, to learn that space of the universe does not have to comply with Euclidean geometry was implicitly to admit that the foundations of Newtonian physics were cracking, or at least made uncertain. The realization dawned that many different geometries are possible, within any of which we can describe the physical cosmos. As the result of absorbing this shock, *conventionalism* was born—an ingenious doctrine of Henri Poincaré and Pierre Duhem who claimed that systems of knowledge we develop do not necessarily describe reality faithfully in a one-to-one way; rather the system of knowledge one develops depends entirely on the system of axioms which one accepts to begin with. We have a great deal of liberty which system of axioms to choose, for instance, while developing geometry. This was an ingenious way of resolving the problem of non-Euclidean geometries.

Conventionalism solved one problem, but it opened up a Pandora's box to many other problems. In particular, it profoundly undermined the very notion of truth as expressed through science. That is to say, it undermined the classical or correspondence notion of truth according to which truth consists of a correspondence between reality R and our description of it D, so that we can claim that science aims at descriptions of reality which are true. Once we admit that the choice of basic concepts and of the conceptual framework is up to us, we, so to speak, slightly unhinge the classical notion of truth. I say "slightly unhinge" because at the time it appeared that the classical edifice of knowledge, as presented by science, could be saved by artful modifications of the framework.

Then problems started to appear in physics, such as radioactivity and a host of other phenomena which were clearly beyond the domain of the Newtonian paradigm.

Those problems were by and large solved by 20th century physics: Einstein's theory of relativity, Bohr's quantum theory, Heisenberg's principle of uncertainty. While we welcomed those specific extensions of physics, we have not fully realized, let alone absorbed and digested, their consequences as they pertain to our theories of knowledge and of mind. True enough, quite a number of philosophical theories were created as the result of the emergence of quantum theory. However, the main problems—the relation of scientific truth to reality and the role of the mind in those ever-new extensions of physics—have been bypassed, neglected, almost ignored.

Let me be emphatic. Since conventionalism emerged (in the second half of the 19th century) we have not come to terms—faithfully, adequately, unequivocally—with the notion of truth and with the notion of reality that science purportedly describes.

While putting forth the proposition that philosophy did not absorb in any depth the consequences of the changes in science, we must not forget Karl Popper. He indeed was so struck with the fact that even the most entrenched scientific theories (such as Newton's) finally fall and are falsified that he decided to build a new epistemology on the grounds of this finding. Popper's distinctive philosophy of science takes the clue from Einstein (as the over-thrower of Newton) and claims that all knowledge is tentative. But at the same time it attempts to salvage and justify the superiority of scientific knowledge over all other forms of knowledge. Although Popper's epistemology admirably meets the challenge of Einstein, it is ill at ease with regard to quantum theory.

Let me emphasize: Popper's philosophy has only attempted to meet the challenge of Einstein vis-a-vis Newton; it did not attempt to make sense of the most recent stages of particle physics. My theory of co-creative mind attempts to meet the challenge of our present understanding as posed by recent extensions in physics and in other domains of knowledge. Thus Popper's main problem was the challenge of Einstein. My main problem is the challenge of the new physics, which shows that the observer and the observed merge, and therefore the traditional notion of objectivity must be abandoned. Popper's response was within the theory of knowledge, or epistemology. My response is within the theory of mind, which to me appears to be the clue to our new understanding.

The cornerstone of scientific theories is for Popper empirical refutability, in other words, the assumption that there is an empirical reality out there which science faithfully describes; and because it does so, we can compare our theories with nature herself. The meaning of refutability rests on the assumption that science *does* describe reality in an unequivocal and faithful way. Although Popper did not give up the classical notion of truth explicitly, he did give it up implicitly. As the result of Thomas Kuhn's reconstruction of science, Popper seemed to have agreed with Kuhn that theories are not refuted in actual scientific practice. Rather, like old soldiers they fade away. Even if Popper did not agree with this specific formulation of Kuhn, he conceded the fact that theories are never *ultimately* refuted. Since the publication of Kuhn's *The Structure of Scientific Revolutions* (1963), Popper has been rather mute about the importance of falsifiability.

My main point is that since the rise of conventionalism we have lost grip of the classical notion of truth and also of the notion of reality that science purportedly *describes*, that is, in the classical sense of the term *describes*. Even the best of the 20th century thinkers such as Popper have been unable to resolve the dilemmas that 20th century knowledge has posed to our comprehension.

When Newtonian physics began to totter and could no longer be seen as expressing unshakable laws of nature, this gave rise to many ad hoc theories in science and in philosophy. With Ernst Mach we observe the shift from the correspondence theory of truth to the coherence theory of truth. Since science could not claim to be the guardian of truth, understood as a faithful description of reality out there, scientists and philosophers decided that perhaps we should consider statements and theories as true insofar as they are coherent with the rest of accepted knowledge.

Out of the many attempts to make sense of the post-Newtonian physics, perhaps the most radical, at least in its conceptual implications, was that of Percy Bridgman who conceived the doctrine of *operationalism*. Operationalism was a radical attempt to avoid any metaphysics, and indeed to avoid the troublesome concept of 'reality.' According to Bridgman, physical concepts need not have their ontological equivalents in the reality outside physics. The meaning of a concept, Bridgman insisted, is a set of operations we perform with it. "Meaning is to be sought in operations," wrote Bridgman in 1934. After that the definitions become increasingly diluted. In 1938 a more liberal definition was provided: "Operations are a 'necessary' but not a 'sufficient' condition for the determination of meanings." This formulation was still weakened in 1952: "The operational aspect is not by any means the only aspect of meaning." There is a considerable discrepancy between the first and the last formulation. Although the scientific concepts were to be characterized by means of operational definitions, the concept of operation has never been clearly defined by Bridgman. It is obvious that Bridgman himself has given up the idea that meanings are to be sought in operations.

This story is well known and one may wonder why I rehearse it here again. For an important reason: to make it quite clear that it was a pervading crisis in the foundation of Western knowledge that brought about those pseudo-solutions like operationalism and the empiricist criterion of meaning. These semantic strategies were taken on face value and gave rise to a host of new theories, including theories of mind. *The Concept of Mind* by Gilbert Ryle, originally published in 1949, is a crowning achievement of the whole epoch, bent on attempting to find salvation through semantics. I will return to Ryle shortly.

Operationalism was not an isolated, obscure doctrine but in many ways epitomized the spirit of the times. Quite independently of Bridgman a group of thinkers who did their philosophy in the coffee houses of Vienna arrived at the celebrated empiricist criterion of meaning, according to which only empirically verifiable statements are meaningful, all others are meaningless, save tautologies or mathematical and logical equivalencies such as $2+2=4$ or $p \cdot q = q \cdot p$. I refer here to the Vienna Circle and the spectacular rise of their philosophy which managed to eclipse nearly all other philosophies in the mid-century.

Also making its career in the early decades of the 20th century was Behaviorism, first in its crude formulation by J. B. Watson, then in its more "sophisticated" version of B. F. Skinner. Behaviorism actually was a doctrine quite apart from the other two. But it had the same purpose: to eliminate everything complex, subtle, and human and reduce it to the stuff of pigeons. This is by no means an exaggeration, for the purpose of the methodology generated by Behaviorism was to study pigeons. And yet, in all seriousness it was extended to the study of human beings. The heyday of Behaviorism and its methodology are now over. It now appears quite *strange* that we could have taken such a crude doctrine so seriously. Yet it was taken seriously.

Behaviorism, operationalism, logical empiricism, and other forms of positivism were all developed within a larger philosophical envelope of the time: ontological materialism, often coupled with atheism. The purpose of nearly all the new "isms" (that somehow signified the Brave New World) was the same: to reduce all other layers and aspects of human existence to inanimate matter.

This is therefore the context for viewing prominent theories of mind of the Anglo-Saxon philosophy of the second half of the 20th century. Ryle's *The Concept of Mind* is a magnificent and scintillating book. Yet, as brilliant as his achievement is, it is but an offering on the altar of the reductionist ethos, one which so impressed itself on our thinking that it renders the mind as a curiously lifeless, uncreative, and unimaginative faculty.

Ryle is admirably lucid about his intentions, as he writes:

104

This book offers what may with reservations be described as a theory of mind. But it does not give new information about minds. We possess already a wealth of information about minds, information which is neither derived from, nor upset by, the arguments of philosophers. The philosophical arguments which constitute this book are intended not to increase what we know about minds, but to rectify the logical geography of the knowledge which we already possess. (*The Concept of Mind*, p. 7.)

The rectification of the logical geography of our knowledge about minds becomes a very labored process, and it finally leads to Ryle's theory of logical types (of mind's activities). The semantic footwork is inventive and brilliant. But the whole venture is simply reductionistic: the idea is not to understand *mind* as it is and as it works, but to reduce it to its observable byproducts. Ryle's is a materialist theory of mind. It is also a behaviorist and operationalist theory, as it tries to avoid the problem of mind by studying outwardly observable behavior. Thus in Ryle we see the synthesis of materialism, operationalism, logical empiricism, and behaviorism. The result is virtuosity in applying the pigeon methodology which obscures real understanding of what mind is.

Ryle is a pivotal point of the materialist-reductionist-operationalist tradition. His work set the tone for the next decades of endless epicycles on the theme of the semantic-materialist theory. This now has become a tradition and quite an industry, sometimes called inquiry into mental concepts—pretending to be in the domain of the theory of mind and purportedly explaining the life of mind, but actually as detached from it as a dry leaf is detached from a healthy, growing tree.

The tradition here outlined was born of the crisis in the foundations of Western knowledge which is still with us. This tradition, perhaps inadvertently, has created a monumental body of distinctions and semantic refinements which contribute but little to our understanding of the world at large. Now if "Scholasticism" describes a body of knowledge which, through its verbal virtuosity, obscures rather than illumines the purposes of our understanding, then the semantic empiricist tradition of the 20th century deserves the name of the New Scholasticism.

The tradition with which I wish to identify myself is one which stems from new physics: the post-Newtonian and post-Einsteinian physics. Philosophically it is the tradition of Whitehead and Teilhard de Chardin. In short, it is the tradition which takes the notion of creative evolution seriously. Before I sketch what I call the ecological theory of mind, let me briefly survey some historical theories of mind.

17
Mind in the Universe of Becoming

The history of Western philosophy is a marvelous tale of human inventiveness and of human follies. Theories of mind are as numerous as theories of reality. But with some singular exceptions these two, mind and reality, are separated from each other and viewed independently of each other. Some pre-Socratic philosophers knew better than that. One of them, Parmenides, said "No mind, no world." In these four words a whole magnificent insight is contained. During earlier centuries and millennia we did not have sufficient knowledge, and also perhaps sufficient courage, to translate this insight into a complete model of Mind/Reality.

Cartesian dualism, which radically separates the mind from the body and mind from nature, has been at the root of many of our misconceptions and quite a few of our dilemmas. In order to overcome this dualism, we must create a unified theory within which mind and reality can be treated as aspects of each other. The evolutionary-transcendental theory of mind, which I shall here present (and which I call, for short, the *ecological* conception of mind), treats mind as co-extensive with reality, and treats reality as a form of mind. This theory draws from the insight of Parmenides, "No mind, no world"; but more importantly, it builds on the conception of man as the custodian and beneficiary of ever new emerging sensitivities.

Before we go into the details of the ecological conception of mind, let us take a brief look at some of the theories of mind which have been most influential in the West, and which still hold sway over our minds.

Empiricism is both a theory of knowledge and a theory of mind. It holds that there is nothing in the intellect that has previously not been in the senses. Mind is conceived here essentially as a *tabula rasa*, a white sheet on which experience writes its designs. The only active role of the mind is that it *allows* experience to write on it. Out of rudimentary experiences first impressions are formed. These impressions are transformed into forms of knowledge. How these transformations of raw experience and of impressions occur has never been explained satisfactorily by empiricism.

Empiricism as a theory of mind is a gross caricature of what is going on in our mind and what we know about the marvels of human comprehension. One wonders *why* it has ever been taken so seriously and, indeed, propagated by intelligent people with zeal and commitment. The main reason for the acceptance of this clearly defective theory, in my opinion, has been ideological: the empiricist theory of the mind removes human knowledge from the authority of the church, and particularly from the church's creeds and dogmas. Empiricism maintains that *everything* is acquired from the physical universe via the senses, thus instructs us that no authority of any sort needs to be obeyed. The only authority is that of our senses.

In the long run the physical universe becomes the only reality which we not only explore but also worship, as all other gods are dethroned; and our senses become not only our authorities, but also our deities. A theory of knowledge, which sought to overcome the overbearing dogmatism of religious orthodoxies has itself become a sterile dogma: not only detrimental to the quest of knowledge which goes beyond the mere physical surface, but also detrimental to the human quest for meaning, which is frustrated by empiricism's insistent claim that there is nothing beyond the reality of the senses. In spite of its numerous defects, empiricism is still holding strong and manifests itself in the oversimplified theories of natural and social science which are still favored in our academia. These theories still reduce the complex and the exquisite to the simple and the physical.

Predating empiricism, but also running parallel to it, we find theories which do not consider mind as a tabula rasa, but which on the contrary attribute to it an active role. Many of these theories claim that mind is endowed with capacities and propensities that are inborn, therefore a priori. These are *rationalist* theories of mind.

Among the rationalist theories of mind at least three should be mentioned: Plato's, Berkeley's, Kant's. Plato envisaged mind as active, but only so far as it recognizes, really 'remembers' the Forms: ideal, incorruptible, unchangeable blueprints to which all objects of our knowledge and indeed all objects of existence must comply. Objects are what they are because ideal Forms predating their existence are embodied in them.

Berkeley's conception of mind is active in the extreme. Bishop Berkeley maintained that "esse percipi," to be is to be perceived. All existence is, in a sense, a figment of our imagination. Things are "brought" into existence through acts of our perception and exist only insofar as we perceive them. The consequence is subjective idealism: there is no reality independent of our perception. This is an ingenious and startling doctrine, particularly when defended by the scintillating mind of Bishop Berkeley, but it makes nonsense of all that we know. It also makes nonsense of evolution itself, especially evolution as striving towards greater and greater complexity, attainment, perfection.

The third type of rationalist theory of mind is that of Emmanuel Kant, which comes closest to the ecological conception of mind, and yet is still far away. Kant reversed the whole process as envisaged by the empiricists. Instead of objects impressing themselves on the mind, Kant claimed that it is the other way around—it is the mind, its specific structure and its specific categories, that are imposed on the objects outside, which are shaped according to the categories of the mind. There is conformity between objects and the mind, but this conformity comes about by the mind imposing its order on things. We perceive a certain order in the outside world and we structure it according to certain regularities because we cannot do otherwise. The structure of our mind continuously impresses itself on the order of reality. The order of reality is really the order of the mind.

Kant claimed that we cannot know the ultimate reality, "things in themselves." We only know the appearances of things. For we structure according to the categories of the mind, but only the appearances of reality. The whole conception of reality is opaque in Kant and indeed one big question mark. There is, as a matter of fact, no room for evolution in the Kantian system, and this was a major reason for the collapse of Kantian philosophy. When non-Euclidian geometries emerged, this shattered Kantian conception of absolute (Euclidian) space, one of the absolute categories of mind. With the progress in physics and mathematical logic, other 'absolute' categories of the mind were undermined.

Kant's major shortcoming was to envisage the mind's categories and indeed mind's structure as fixed and absolute. In postulating an active role for the mind, and in claiming that the world is shaped and determined by the categories of our knowledge, his influence has been great and lasting. *His* active mind was second to none.

We should add, parenthetically, that Kant's heritage has continued (though in a changed idiom) throughout the 19th century and throughout the present century. What Kant attributed to the mind—the shaping and determining of reality—various other thinkers attributed to language. First came Poincaré with his ingenious conception of conventionalism; then came Ajdukiewicz, Benjamin Lee Whorf, and Quine, who radicalized Poincaré's conventionalism; and, more recently, Chomsky has crusaded for the recognition of man as a language animal. Each of them has recognized language as a co-definer of knowledge and of reality. Each was close to seeing that reality and mind co-define each other.

From these theories of mind, both empiricist and rationalist, I wish to distinguish the evolutionary transcendental theory of mind, which I call the ecological conception of mind, in order to separate it from other would-be evolutionary theories. This ecological conception of mind is much closer to rationalist theories than to empiricist ones. The hallmark of the ecological theory is that it recognizes mind not only as active but as co-creative: as made not only of abstract powers of reasoning, but also of the sensitivities of the entire body.

The rationalists were on the right track, but they lacked the evolutionary dimension. Hence their conception of mind was constrained and ultimately ridden with irresolvable dilemmas, which neither Plato, nor Berkeley, nor Kant could escape.

The ecological theory of mind wants to make sense of Parmenides' insight: "No mind, no world"; it wants to make sense of the mind as a product of evolution unfolding and of that part of our intellectual endowment which has to do with the acquisition of new sensitivities.

Let us return to our earlier story of the evolutionary ascent. When the first amoebas started to articulate themselves from the original sea of the primordial, organic soup, this was at once a triumph of life ascending and a triumph (still muted at the time) of consciousness arising. For amoebas started to *react* to the environment in a deliberate and semiconscious manner.

From this point on, the evolutionary tale is one of augmentation of consciousness and the continuous acquisition of new *sensitivities*, through which organisms react to the environment in ever more knowing and purposeful ways. As their sensitivities multiply, organisms elicit more and more from the environment: *they draw from reality in proportion to their ability to receive it and transform it.* At this point, we can see that their reality was outlined by the nature and scope of their consciousness and their sensitivities—we might even say by the nature of their "mind."

There is, therefore, an intimate relationship between our total evolutionary endowment in terms of consciousness, all the knowing powers we possess, and the nature of reality we construct, receive, and recognize. We simply cannot envisage, find, and discover in reality more than our senses, our intellect, our sensitivities—and whatever other evolutionary endowments we possess—allow us to find and see. *The more sensitive and knowing we become, the richer and larger becomes our reality.* When we say "our," we do not mean in the sense of idiosyncratic, subjective perception. We mean the capacity of the species. What is beyond the mind of the species may be reality *in potentio*, but it is reality beyond us, not for us; it does not yet exist for us. God's perfect reality may very well exist for God, but it does not yet exist for us.

While receiving reality or any aspect of it, the mind (according to the ecological theory) always processes it. In processing it, the mind actively transforms reality. Let us reflect on the meaning of the two expressions: "processing reality" and "transforming reality." They are both fundamentally inadequate. For they suggest that there is such a thing as an autonomous reality "out there" to which the mind applies itself and on which it works. Such a picture is fundamentally misconceived. There isn't such a thing as *reality as it is*, which the mind visits and on which it works. Reality is always given within the mold of the mind which comprehends it, that is, in the acts of comprehension, which are at the same time the acts of transformation. We have no idea whatsoever what reality could be like *as it is*, because whenever we think of it and behold it (in whatever manner), reality is invariably presented to us, *as it has been transformed by our cognitive faculties.*

The organism's interaction with reality is a process whereby by participating in reality, the organism invariably articulates it. Reality is never given to the organism

112

(human or otherwise) *except* in forms of interactions; thus, in the form of continuous transformations specific to a given organism. We never *just* receive reality.

Mind is part of the real. It is a fragment of evolution unfolding itself. But it is a rather special fragment: once it has emerged, it acts as a transforming instrument. It "bends" and "refracts" reality according to its peculiar laws, propensities, and faculties. Mind is part of reality among other parts; but it is also *apart* from reality as it acts as the mirror of all reality. This double nature of mind accounts for many linguistic perplexities which arise when we talk of "mind as the stuff of reality." By saying that it is "of reality" and "within reality," we expect to find a slot whereby the mind can be shown as existing "objectively" among other things. But mind is not this kind of thing. To find it, you have to have a mind. Mind is finding itself when we find it among other things of reality. Any situating of mind in reality is in effect situating reality within itself.

Hence, the ecological theory is at the same time an interactive theory of mind. Reality and mind constantly interact with each other. There is no other way of grasping reality but through the mind, which is continually shaping reality. To say that mind shapes and co-creates reality is not the same as saying that all reality is created by mind, a figment of our imagination; we part company with Bishop Berkeley.

In its evolutionary development the mind has not only been continually transformed but continually transforming. The mind, as I have argued throughout, is not to be limited to its one layer embodied in our abstract logical capacities, but must be seen as the total capacity of the organism to react intelligently and purposefully.

The reality for the amoeba has been something less than for the fish, and still less than for the human being. The richness and multifariousness of the experience of reality is in proportion to the organism's capacity to receive and decipher it. The more primitive the capacities (or to put it in another way, the more primitive the mind), the more primitive the furniture and experience of reality. The more versatile and exquisite the mind, the more versatile the reality and the richer the experience of it.

We may put it in a paradoxical way: *the organism receives from reality as much as it puts into it.* It "enriches" and transforms reality through its capacity of articulation, through its versatile mind. The notion of God (conceived as a being capable of everything, thus omnipotent) makes perfect sense in this evolutionary scheme. If there were a being whose mind is infinitely creative and thus capable of transforming the world (reality) at will, this being would be God. Reality for God, however, would be a strange thing: not a permanent, fixed realm, but something that is constantly created and recreated, a rather uncomfortable notion for us earthlings, who must be rooted in permanent realms.

From these considerations a general conclusion would seem to follow: the more creative the person, the more impermanent his or her environment (reality). If mental breakdowns are tantamount to instability of one's reality, then it would seem that the more sensitive the person, the more prone he or she will be to those breakdowns—because of the instability of his or her reality. Geniuses have been notoriously unstable. Highly creative persons must be either unstable in their mental health or unusually comfortable with change and lack of structure. It is a disturbing notion that God, being the genius supreme, might be unstable, and our problems might be residue of this instability.

The wonder and mystery of the mind in evolution is its capacity to enlarge reality, as mind itself grows and transforms itself. The mind is but a product of evolution unfolding, but it is the most extraordinary product. It is the light which penetrates and illumines. The mind, being part of the real, sends a beam across to other parts of the real and, by illuminating them, brings them back to the source of the light—the mind itself. By illuminating the darkness and bringing it to light, the mind elevates nonbeing into being. Vision and the seeing cannot be separated from the eye. What the eye is to the act of seeing, the mind is to the act of comprehending reality.

We are an aspect of the universal mind or the total mind, and our limitations reflect the limitations of this larger mind. We can become much brighter, but only if the *total mind* as developed by the whole of humanity (through evolution) becomes much larger and brighter.

The conception of mind as co-extensive with reality explains why we cannot suddenly increase our mind tenfold, fivefold, or even twofold. Our mind is limited by the boundaries of reality co-created by it, is limited by the scope of human knowledge, by the nature of human understanding. If there are individuals who have radically transcended these boundaries, more likely than not we have locked them up in lunatic asylums. He who radically transcends the scope of his mind, radically transcends the scope of his reality. We have all had an experience in which suddenly our mind is ablaze and reality around us dramatically changes. But there are biological and psychological limits to this process of transformation: by broadening and changing the nature of reality around us, we uproot ourselves, we derascinate ourselves from the reality we have been rooted in; we lose our security, our sense of belonging; we become, in a sense, schizophrenic. There are, therefore, biological and psychological limits to what we call a radical expansion of the mind.

How does the expansion of the mind occur within the scope of the universal mind or the mind of the species? It is like climbing unconquered mountains. Before the north face of the Eiger was conquered, it was deemed unconquerable. Once it was scaled, it has become yet *another* route. The psychological curtain of impossibility has been removed. The mind has learned that this is now a possibility, and within the sphere of 'reality.' Before Mount Everest was conquered, it was the ultimate human frontier. Once it had been climbed, it became yet another mountain.

The mind is not the slayer of the real. It is the illuminator of the real. Without the mind there is darkness, and there is no sense whatsoever with which we can talk about reality, even through our silence. There is no way of grasping what is out there except through the net of our mind. "Out there" is always an aspect of the "within" (the mind), that is, as far as our comprehension goes; and what is beyond our comprehension *is* beyond our comprehension.

The ecological theory of mind is not an expression of old-fashioned idealism which denies or mystifies reality. It is rather an expression of *supra-realism*. For it accounts for all the stages of the real in its evolutionary unfolding. It makes sense of the reality of the amoeba, of the reality of primitive cultures, of the reality of the scientific culture, of the reality of esoteric traditions; each is weaving its reality according to the capacities of its mind.

The objectivized mind is one specific crystallization of our evolutionary journey. The scientific view of reality is one specific way of its reception and its transformation. Yes, the reception of reality in the scientific key transforms reality—through the numerous filters which science places between us and the real "out there" (which always must be put in inverted commas because there isn't any real *out there*). Some of these filters are sophisticated indeed, such as Schrödinger's equations and other mathematical symbols through which we filter and express reality.

Mind is the glory of evolution, and evolution is safeguarding mind so that it does not become a dreary computing machine. The ecological theory of mind restores the power and place of mind in the universe of becoming. To be alive as a human being affords an enthralling spectacle because we are constantly entertained by the theatre of the mind.

18
Prigogine and Dialectics: Uphill from Entropy

Heraclitus is one of the grandfathers of Western thought. His heritage is as profound as it is shrouded in mystery. He is the father of dialectical thinking. After three centuries of being dominated by mechanistic thinking we are now returning to dialectical thinking. To understand evolution is to understand change. To understand change is to understand the dialectics of becoming, which is not a simple linear process.

The recurrent question with regard to evolution, and particularly in relation to large open systems such as biological organisms, has been: "How does it happen?" Albert Szent-Gyorgyi, an indefatigable explorer of the mysteries of life (and a Nobel Laureate in bio-chemistry) has suggested that the drive towards greater and more complex order may be a fundamental principle of nature. The relentless drive for greater order is an expression of *syntropy* of life, which is the process opposite to *entropy*.

The capacity of life to organize itself in ever more intricate wholes cannot, in his opinion, be the result of random mutations; the wholes of which living organisms are made are too exquisite for that. To suggest that an intricate whole (a living organism) can be improved by random mutation of one link sounds to me (he argued) like saying that you could improve a Swiss watch by bending one of its wheels or axis. *"To get a better watch, you must change all the wheels simultaneously to make a*

good fit again." (Italics mine.) Szent-Gyorgyi was not the
first to emphasize the importance of complexity in living
system; he was in fact following in the footsteps of
Teilhard.

Szent-Gyorgyi's idea was taken up in the 70s by Ilya
Prigogine, a Belgian physical chemist of Russian origin.
Prigogine's term *dissipative structures* is a dubious
semantic invention; it pollutes language with unpleasant
neologisms. However, the concept is important. Now, dissipative structures are open systems in dynamic
equilibrium, the very ones (including ourselves) which
are the glory of evolution transforming itself. Among these
systems should be included, not only biological organisms,
but also such human creations as cities—combating
entropy through an intricate series of dynamic patterns
which actually *enhance* life.

Open systems in dynamic equilibrium can be seen as
flowing wholeness. The equilibrium is constantly re-
established, as in an airplane. Biological organisms, while
alive, are hardly ever in a state of stasis. The state of
stasis could be called dynamic stability. Dynamic stability
would mean galloping entropy, sliding towards death.

Prigogine's distinctive contribution to our thinking
on evolution is the introduction of the idea of *evolutionary
stress* and its consequences. When organisms and other
open systems cannot take evolutionary pressure any more,
the result often is that, instead of collapsing and disinte-
grating, they actually reorganize in new wholes of a higher
order. The system upgrades itself, so to speak, and
escapes the pressure by making *more* of itself rather than
less. Szent-Gyorgyi's image of an improved Swiss watch is
evident here: a new and better whole created as a result of
reorganization of all the parts under evolutionary stress.

True to the spirit of Teilhard, Prigogine maintains
that the more complex and intricate the structure, the
greater and more coherent will be the next level of organization and complexity. More importantly, while changing
their nature by imploding into themselves, those new
systems change the dynamics of things: "the nature of the

118

laws of nature changes." The net result is life devouring entropy. To repeat: under evolutionary stress, a complex system does not crumble into entropic chaos, but on the contrary produces structures which are ever more effective in combating entropy. The idea is expressed in a different language, but its import is very close to the spirit of Teilhard.

Prigogine's theory answers at least two problems. One is: why and how do ever more organized and capable systems emerge out of less organized and less capable ones? Evolutionary stress is a creative modus of life.

The other problem which Prigogine's theory attempts to answer, at least partly, is one connected with so-called gaps in the evolutionary record: under evolutionary stress, organisms do not adapt gradually, but make a jump to a new and higher level of organization. This alone would explain so-called gaps in evolution. For evolution is not a gradual process but a discontinuous one, not unlike the process we witness in the history of science within which one paradigm replaces another in a dramatic discontinuous manner, reorganizing the entire body of knowledge in its wake. Gaps in evolution are small bits of "paradigm shift."

Prigogine's theory of evolutionary change has a look of one flowing river, but like a river, it is made of many tributaries. These tributaries are Teilhard de Chardin, Ludwig von Bertalanffy, Albert Szent-Gyorgyi, Thomas Kuhn, Kazimierz Dabrowski and Fritjof Capra. From Teilhard undoubtedly comes the idea that the more integrated and connected the system the more resilient it is in terms of entropy, and also the idea that the genius of life lies in its ability to progress from the simple to the complex, for in this progression it combats entropy. Life eats entropy by the uniqueness of its organization.

From Bertalanffy comes the idea of open and closed systems, which he elaborated in 1948. He pointed out in his various publications on general systems theory that physics and chemistry cannot understand open systems, particularly open biological systems. For to understand

119

these systems means to understand life, while physics and chemistry deal with dead matter.

From Albert Szent-Gyorgyi comes the idea that "to get a better watch, you must change all the wheels simultaneously." In open systems which are under evolutionary stress, their parts reorganize themselves into a new whole, but on a new level of a higher order or organization.

From Thomas Kuhn (*The Structure of Scientific Revolutions*) comes the idea of the paradigm and the paradigm shift: significant developments in science and elsewhere do not occur in a linear manner, by accretion, but happen dramatically: at crucial junctures the whole in its entirety is switched into another whole which is organized differently. The old paradigm (the old organization) is negated and creatively transcended.

From the Polish psychologist, Kazimierz Dabrowski, comes the theory of *positive disintegration*, outlined in the mid-1960s (see *Positive Disintegration*, 1964; *Personality Shaping Through Positive Disintegration*, 1967). According to this theory, we as human beings do not develop by means of accretion in a linear fashion. Instead, the transition from one phase to another is nothing short of traumatic: we undergo a positive disintegration of our earlier personality out of which emerges a reintegrated new whole. The early stages of human development, before we are formed in later life, follow a distinctly dialectical pattern: discontinuities and partial disintegrations are natural and inevitable—for the sake of reintegration on a higher level.

From physicists like Werner Heisenberg, Fritjof Capra, and others comes the idea that physics at its creative edge in the second half of the 20th century has left behind the deterministic, mechanistic model and has become something much more inspiring and fascinating, like an eternal dance of Shiva. The state of subatomic physics, particularly at its cutting edge, encourages us to think that radical shifts in our perceptions and conceptions are not only possible but necessary. The discontinuous picture of the universe, in which new forms of organizations are created and recreated de novo, is powerfully re-affirmed.

Ilya Prigogine may well be startled to find his ideas traced back to so many predecessors. Let me hasten to add, therefore, that some of these ideas and influences may be merely implicit in his work and perhaps not even consciously. We are not undertaking here the reconstruction of Prigogine's cast of mind, but rather a reconstruction of the whole cultural formation that enables his type of mind to emerge.

Now there is yet another strand in Prigogine's theory which I have not mentioned but which lurks in the background. This is dialectical materialism and its laws of dialectics. Communism is still much feared in the West, particularly in the U.S. Because of this, we tend to shy away from everything that is connected with Marxism, including its theory of economics, and including its philosophy and its *dialectical* way of viewing all development in society and evolution. Whether it is because of Prigogine's Russian background or his general susceptibility to ideas of promise, there is no question that he is not only aware of the so-called laws of dialectics, but that he creatively uses them for his own theory.

Our times are bound in paradoxes. While the Soviet thinkers *preach* the dialectical mode, their actual practice is that of dogmatic and petrified thinking—a constant repetition of Marxist dogmas. In the hands of some Western thinkers such as Prigogine, dialectics once again becomes a tool of creative reconstruction.

Emphasizing the crucial role of time in evolutionary processes, Prigogine is acutely aware of the "laws of change," of the fact that "as long as we had only those naive views of time and physics and chemistry, science had little to say to art." If we bring the time dimension to the evolutionary process, and if we become aware of the laws of change and incorporate them in our thinking, science can be enriched so that we shall arrive at "a human physics" which is relevant to the lives of individuals and of society as well. Prigogine's program is to create such

121

a "human physics." I wonder whether we should aim at such a thing, for physics will always attempt to physicalize.

The vicissitudes of dialectical thinking are fascinating. With Heraclitus and the pre-Socratic philosophers the dialectical comprehension of reality is not only apparent but also pronounced within Western intellectual tradition. From Plato on, and particularly after Aristotle, this dialectical tradition becomes submerged. It never dies out, however. Hegel resuscitates it in a sweeping manner. Then Marx with Engels blows it up still more: the importance of dialectics and dialectical thinking becomes grossly exaggerated. A new branch of inquiry called *dialectical logic*, with its special laws, is created; or at least outlined. The laws of this logic are supposed to have superseded the laws of Aristotelian or formal logic, often called bourgeois logic.

There was, in point of fact, a lot of nonsense written on the subject of the superiority of dialectical logic over formal logic in the Marxist literature up until roughly the mid-1950s. Then Polish Marxists, who were better trained in the rudiments of logic and semantics and altogether more sophisticated philosophically, settled the issue by arguing that one must not mix these two kinds of logic as they apply to two different realms. Dialectical logic is applicable to the explanation of *processes* in development; formal logic is applicable to the realm of formulated thought. One does not contradict the other; their universes of discourse are different. From this time on, the claims concerning the superiority of dialectical logic over formal logic have decidedly waned.

Now, as the result of our creative reconstruction of the nature of science (Popper, Bertalanffy, Kuhn, Feyerabend), and as the result of our creative reconstruction of the nature of evolution (Teilhard, Dobzhansky, Szent-Gyorgyi, etc.), we have gained a new perspective on dialectics and dialectical ways of looking at reality. In this process Prigogine represents a synthesis. He represents a new level of articulation of our thinking on dialectics; a new level of *dialectical* thinking; therefore a new level of understanding of the evolutionary process.

This new wave of dialectical thinking is but a belated recognition of the Heraclitean tradition in Western thought: "You cannot step into the same river twice." With the recognition of open systems in dynamic equilibrium as crucial to our understanding of the creative modus of evolution, we are recognizing the primacy of process over facts; the primacy of laws governing dynamic patterns over static laws governing inanimate matter; the primacy of the living and changing over the molecular and dead; the primacy of the active and co-creative mind over a merely receptive and passive one.

The creative elan of evolution sooner or later was bound to redirect our minds from the tedious, repetitive, deterministic, and mechanistic towards the creative and emergent, both in evolution and in our lives. We are clearly on the creative and emergent crest. Our courage and imagination must come to our aid so that we do not miss the momentum.

19
Responsibility

Responsibility is one of the most peculiar concepts of
our language—and of our moral universe. It is very hard to
define, even harder to live without. There is no logical
necessity or even natural necessity to assume responsibility. Yet we render ourselves less than human when we do
not do so. Responsibility is one of those invisible human
forces—like will power—for which there is no logical or
natural necessity but without which human history is
inconceivable.

In the consumptive society, we want to escape from
responsibility, assuming that without it our lives will be
easier and better, whereas in fact our lives become
shallower and cheaper. Like faith, responsibility enhances
the variety of our existence when we possess it, or
diminishes us when we lack it. What blood is to the body,
responsibility is to the spirit.

Responsibility is a precondition of morality; it is thus
a moral category. Responsibility is a precondition of understanding the world in its totality; it is thus a cognitive
category. In short, responsibility is part of our moral
make-up and also a part of the definition of being human.
We are confused about the nature of responsibility and our
own responsibilities mainly because we are confused
about our relationship to the cosmos and our moral obliga-
tions to the human family.

In the world of pre-scientific societies, the physical

order of the world is an aspect of the moral; the moral order is part of the larger cosmic order. The perception of the pre-scientific man is so structured that he sees in the surrounding world—in the cycles of nature, in the way physical reality manifests itself—the confirmation of the moral order which his world-view postulates. The outer world and the inner world are in harmony, aspects of each other.

Now this harmony is undermined, if not entirely in pieces, in the scientific world-view in which the physical world and the inner world are separated from each other, and more often than not exclude each other. There is no unity between our inner world and the outer cosmos, between the moral law and the natural law. As the result our sense of responsibility is confused. The way to the restoration of our sense of responsibility, which is part of the restoration of our inner harmony, is through the creation of a new cosmology within which the moral order and the physical order are aspects of each other, or at least united in a comprehensive framework which makes sense of each. One of the tasks of this book is to suggest this unitary cosmology. (See, especially, last chapters.)

We are evolution conscious of itself, and the cosmos is our home. The order we find in the cosmos is neither given to us a priori (created by God, therefore absolute and unalterable), nor is it entirely subjective (the product of the imagination of individuals, therefore totally relative). Rather, order *acquires* objectivity in the course of evolution which, through the capacity of the human mind to create order, affirms itself in structures of increasing complexity. On the level of Homo sapiens, evolution predisposes the human mind to create trans-subjective values, to establish moral codes, to set up social contracts—as well as to conceive of responsibility as an important attribute of human existence.

Our destiny in this context is to be aware of the responsibility which we carry for the future continuation of evolution. Our great problem is that *the sense of responsibility is unevenly distributed among humans.*

There are some individuals who consider responsibility an unbearable burden. Hence their recurrent question: Why should I carry this cross on my shoulders? Why should I carry more than my share? Why should I be responsible while others are not?

For Socrates and Plato sin is almost an intellectual category: the result of ignorance. Enlightenment is therefore a precondition of virtuous life. Consequently, the process of upbringing and education is one which is identified with the search for enlightenment; truth is in itself a virtue. Goodness, truth, and beauty have their source in enlightenment. Their denial leads to ignorance, which is the source of sin. Another source of sin is to forsake our responsibility.

To be a human being is to live in a state of responsibility. When we are unable to be responsible or voluntarily give up our responsibility, we are, in a sense, annihilating our status as human beings. Human existence oscillates between those two poles: the sense of responsibility, on the one hand, and an attempt to escape from it, on the other. Those oscillations are the cause of our continuous inner struggle.

Those "chosen by the gods" are those who possess a sense of responsibility bordering on obsession, like the Buddha or Jesus. "Forsaken by the gods" are those who are void of the sense of responsibility—even for their own lives. Great spiritual leaders of mankind, as well as great social and political leaders, are stigmatized with an enhanced sense of responsibility.

The sense of responsibility is not limited to the great of this world; it is known to everybody. For what is the awareness of "the wasted life" if not the recognition that each of us is a carrier of responsibility which goes beyond the boundaries of our little egos and our daily struggles.

Responsibility, seen in the larger cosmic plan, is a late acquisition of evolution. It comes about as consciousness becomes self-consciousness, and furthermore as self-consciousness (in attempting to refine itself) takes upon itself the moral cause: the burden of responsibility for the rest. Responsibility so conceived is a form of altruism. The tendency to escape from responsibility is a purely biological impulse, a self-serving gesture, a form of egoism. Therefore, those two tendencies, the altruistic (accepting the responsibility for all) and egoistic (escaping from it into the shell of our own ego), are continually fighting each other within us. And each of us knows the agony of this fight.

When we observe the lives of great men, the lives that are outstanding and fulfilled, we cannot help noticing that they were invariably inspired by an enhanced sense of responsibility. Those who sacrificed themselves in the name of this responsibility did not have the sense of a wasted life. Their example is received as something noble and inspiring. The sense of responsibility is now built into our psychic structure as an attribute of human existence and a positive force. The negation of this force is sin, because it represents the betrayal of the great evolutionary heritage which brought us about and of which we are always aware, if only dimly.

The smallness or greatness of a person can be measured by the degree of responsibility he or she is capable of exercising for his or her own life, for the lives of others, for everything there is. Small infants and the mentally ill are outside the compass of humanity precisely because they are not capable of exercising responsibility, either for their lives or for the lives of others. They are beyond good and evil, beyond sin and virtue, beyond constraints and delights that unify the human family.

Though fundamental to the core of our existence, the very word "responsibility" (within the Protestant culture) is dreaded as a heavy burden. However, when seen as enlarging our spiritual domain, responsibility is a force that continually elevates us. "Responsibility" is a word that has wings. We must be prepared to fly on them.

Responsibility is at the same time a cognitive category and a moral one: cognitive because it enlightens us as to who we are in the plan of all there is; moral because it *inspires* us to be what we are, and be more than we are.

The traditional questions What is man? Who am I? are both cognitive and moral questions. They are concerned not only with the description of man as he is. They indirectly asked what man ought to be, that is, in order to be worthy to be called human being.

The struggle against evil is so often the struggle against oneself, the struggle against the prison of one's own shell which wants to keep us in the narrow confines of our egoism. When simple people talk about Satan inspiring them to evil, most of them want to escape their responsibility in the name of satisfying their own egoism.

Whether Satan is conceived as an outside being interfering with our inner lives, or whether he is only an aspect of our inner struggle is of no importance. Satan signifies negative responsibility. God signifies infinite responsibility. Man signifies limited responsibility. Satan is a symbol of the destructive power which attempts to destroy the attainment of our spirit and indirectly the attainment of evolution. The traditional moral codes, through giving us commandments concerning human behavior, are props enabling us to lead lives within the compass of responsibility.

To be human is to live in the state of responsibility. However, through the systematic separation of human beings from the cycles of nature, as well as through the process of delegating important decisions to experts, contemporary technology has been systematically disengaging us from life. Our lives have been made increasingly disconnected, atomized, and trivialized. This particular aspect of present technology makes it more detrimental to the future of the human race than any particular technological disaster. (I am, for the moment, disregarding the destruction of eco-habitats and human societies through excessive reliance upon the machine.)

Responsibility and technology must, at this time in history, be considered vis-a-vis each other. Technology which systematically deprives us of responsibility (by delegating everything to experts) represents the victory of evil. For if everything is done for us, if we cannot exercise

128

our responsibility, we are no longer human.

God is the one for whom nothing is done. God does everything. And His responsibility is infinite. The closer we are to God, the more responsibility we exercise; the less responsibility we exercise, the further away we are from God, and from our own humanity. Whether we look at the issue theologically or existentially, *responsibility* is the cornerstone of our status as human and spiritual beings.

Places like Arcosanti, Auroville, and Findhorn should be hailed, for they not only attempt to restore lopsided ecological balances; they also represent salutary attempts to restore human dignity and human purpose by bringing back responsibility to human beings. Decentralized movements should be hailed, for they represent the restoration of human responsibility. Every creative act should be hailed for it represents an expression of human responsibility. Let us be mindful that responsibility implies a sense of the good. "Creating" a bigger bomb is a pathology, not true creativity, for creativity is life-enhancing. When you create you are responsibility incarnate!

20
Education and Self-Lobotomization

"The direction in which education starts a man will determine his future life." (Plato) Our lives are determined by the spectacles our education forces upon us; and then we have no choice but to view the natural world and the human world through these lenses. Each process of education is a little laboratory for living. Yet the technological culture has pushed the idea of the laboratory to such an extreme that when brought into this laboratory we end up estranged from life and not prepared for it.

The virtue of abstract thinking is a virtue indeed—until it is pushed so far that it eclipses other modes of thinking and other forms of sensitivity. Then the human being, subjected to the continuous rigors of this thinking, becomes a machine for computing and abstracting. The education that leads us astray from the human path amounts to the process of self-lobotomization.

There is nothing wrong with the idea of the laboratory. Evolution has created a wonderful laboratory for itself in the bosom of nature. Indeed, evolution as such is one huge laboratory, and each of us is actually evolution's little laboratory. But the dialectic of nature is subtle and complex. When this complexity is radically simplified, we destroy the cycles of nature; we also impoverish ourselves by impoverishing the modes of our comprehension and the range of our perceptions. In trying to outwit nature, we are outwitting ourselves.

In attempting to accelerate the evolutionary process wisely, we are at one with it and we serve it. In thoughtless reduction of the complexities of nature to naive simplicities of reductionist science, we serve no one but the angel of death. The purpose of the laboratory of nature is to enhance what is, not to reduce it, to create diversity, not homogeneity. Education which undermines this diversity and which creates smothering homogeneity is nothing short of the process of self-lobotomization. Lobotomized people have difficulties in their interactions with nature; in their interactions with other people; in finding peace within themselves. There is a clear relationship between our overemphasis on rigorous, scientific, abstract, objectivized, clinical education on the one hand and our existential dilemmas and social crises on the other.

This point must be emphasized: if a people impoverish their minds to the point of crippling their comprehension by drastically narrowing the range of their sensitivities, then they will not see the depth and ramifications of their dilemmas. If the Western mind is indeed lobotomized through its education, then it may very well miss the point that its crucial dilemmas are not economic and technological but moral, and spiritual. The root cause is the loss of human meaning.

Modes of education are translated into modes of thinking, and modes of thinking are translated into modes of living. This also works in the opposite direction: modes of living affect modes of thinking, which in turn generate corresponding modes of perception and interaction with the world. Thus the American Indian of the 19th century, while *educated* by the rhythms and subtleties of nature, was extremely alert to natural phenomena; he treated nature reverentially; his mind was continually open to the wonders of nature. He was an altogether different *being* from the white-coated research scientist whose mind has been hardened by analytical scrutiny, who spends endless hours watching figures rather than blossoming trees. He is sensitive only to cold facts. Can we blame him for his emotional deadness? Can we blame him for his existential anguish? Let us be aware that deep down there is deep anguish.

Our being and our thinking form an integral unity. We cannot remain loving and compassionate if our thinking is dominated by the cold universe of figures. The present system of education, as practiced in the West, must be re-vitalized to include more human values so that the essence of being human is not abolished. The recent outcry about the inadequacy of the American system of education is a recognition of only a surface layer of the problem. Evolution has not created us as disembodied minds to be governed by logic alone, but endowed us with an extraordinary array of emotional, somatic, spiritual, and aesthetic needs. We want a system of education for the complete person, not for the crippled one. We shall have to create such a system, even if this means abolishing the present system.

21
Of Secular and Transcendental Imagination

All decaying cultures, cultures which have lost larger visions of life and the purpose of their pursuit, tend to embrace escapist philosophies such as hedonism, narcissism, stoicism, and nihilism. Such was the case with the decaying Greek culture (which actually invented all those decadent *isms*). Such was the case with the decaying Roman culture. And such is the case with the present Western culture. Although the Western world has never been more powerful in terms of its capacity for destruction, spiritually and morally it is at a low ebb. The nihilism of present Western culture is the product of its impotence.

Now, while stoicism is an expression of resignation confronted bravely and without any escapist hatches, hedonism is an expression of resignation modified by withdrawal into the existential sanctuary of one's senses. Nihilism, on the other hand, is an expression of despair combined with an inner rage and anger at the world, which ultimately is anger at ourselves for not doing any better than we actually do.

Neither narcissism nor hedonism nor especially nihilism can be seriously entertained in the long run. No human society, let alone the human race, can be built on the foundations of despair or trivial self-indulgence. The ethic of hope, which is the ethic of life, is the prerequisite of life alive. In order to hope and build an ethics on it, we have to believe—in things that transcend the frailties of our daily life and the vulgarities of our present commercial world. Faith is an important part of our make-up: one of the attributes of our humanity in us; one of our capacities enabling us to make something of ourselves. Religious people have always known it. Our secular civilization seems to have forgotten.

Let us look at the situation historically. In the 14th and 15th centuries, medieval Europe appeared to be spent and exhausted. However, out of the agonies of the battered Roman Church emerged the Renaissance. Quite miraculously, Europe started to explode with new energy. The resplendent Renaissance inspired by Pythagorean visions, however, gave way to the age of science and, more importantly, to Secular Imagination, with its cult of consumption. There were some good reasons for that, but ultimately it remains a mystery why the West, so rich in imagination before, gave birth to its barren Secular Imagination. This Secular Imagination has, in time, become the master of human destinies, not only in Europe, but the world over; and, in fact, it became the straitjacket that inhibits human lives and mutilates societies and cultures.

In the scriptures of all the religions it is said that "man does not live by bread alone." Yet, possessed by visions of Utopia on earth, possessed by Secular Imagination, which itself became a deity as it promised salvation here on earth, we have plunged with an endless verve and great inventiveness to harness all that was to be harnessed. In the process, we have discovered that this form of salvation was an illusion; and we have also discovered that in pursuing this illusion we have made our lives peculiarly empty.

We have discovered, perhaps too late, that Secular Imagination has produced as its byproduct the value-vacuum, whose consequences are numerous and lamentable: social strife, existential anguish, violence and terrorism, and environmental devastation. If there are no values to hold human beings together, there are no values to hold societies together. If there are no values which make some things sacred, everything is profane and becomes a commodity—an object of exploitation.

In a nutshell, the plight of the Western mind and the nihilism of Western culture is not the result of the mental exhaustion of the West. Far from it. If anything, the West has got only too much of its restless, expansive energy; its plight is due to crippling ideals and the narrow visions which Secular Imagination has brought upon us, and which has finally resulted in the dwarfed conception of man called *homo consumerist*.

Goethe and Blake may have been among the last two men who saw what was coming: the tyranny of the crippled vision. But even their authority and their prophetic visions could not stop the relentless chariot of Secular Imagination. The luminous minds of Dostoevsky and Nietzsche were reduced to voices of despair. Their visions turned out to be an anticipation of Kafka. The Nietzsches and the Rilkes were run over by the chariot of material progress.

That a man of Nietzsche's genius and sensitivity, and of his profound knowledge and understanding, would endorse the idea of the death of God—which was grist to the mill of materialists—is in itself an omen of the blindness of the entire epoch. Perhaps Nietzsche did not actually *endorse* the death of God. But his anticipation of what was to happen greatly contributed to the way things did happen. The lesson from this is as follows: do not share your gloomy visions with others for fear that you may prompt others to make them into a reality.

The voices and the visions of Marx and of Engels and of Feuerbach had to prevail, as they were an extension of the spirit of Secular Imagination which seemed to be crying at the time: "Give me time, give me another century, and I will make the entire world an oasis of prosperity, satisfaction, and happiness."

And another century has passed. And Secular Imagination has collapsed and is now entirely bankrupt. Whether you take its Western embodiment as expressed in capitalism-cum-individualism, or whether you take its Communist variant as expressed by socialism-cum-

communalism—the howling emptiness of Secular
Imagination reverberates agonizingly in our individual and
social lives. We are dazzlingly rich in everything, except
that our lives are empty.

All the forms of nihilism (of present Western culture) can
be traced back to its roots, to Secular Imagination, which
does not recognize gods other than man himself. The
idolatry of man who becomes God (and a rather savage God
for that matter) is the cause of our disrespect for other
creatures of nature, for nature herself, for greater powers
in the cosmos, for other human beings, and finally for
ourselves.

Ultimately our problem is not economic, not even
cultural, but metaphysical, religious, eschatological: by
envisaging limited goals for man's existence, by narrowing
the perspectives of man's life, we have limited the scope
and perverted the meaning of human existence.

Our metaphysics has been reduced to physics. Whether
you call it physicalism or logical empiricism, the result is
the same: the rich structure of man's transcendental
scaffoldings has been reduced to its physical bricks and
mortars. The result is spiritual starvation and the depriva-
tion of a variety of other aspects of human existence.
Starved of real spiritual substance, human beings turn to
substitutes and pseudo-products. The recent explosion of
cults and quackery of all sorts is the result of our spiritual
hunger. They resulted indirectly from our rationality
which was too constraining, thus suffocating, thus in-
ducing people to seek 'liberation' in whatever form.

Metaphysics that reduces itself to physics brings about
its own demise. The end of metaphysics which logical
empiricists postulated, and the end of philosophy which
Heidegger acknowledged, were the acts of philosophical
capitulation vis-a-vis Secular Imagination. Under the
banner of "the end of metaphysics" a lot of shallow and
bad metaphysics has been practiced. Metaphysics can
never be dead as long as human beings are alive and searching for the meaning of their lives, and are puzzled by
the wonders of the world. Metaphysics can, however, be

136

perverted by being reduced to physics or economics.

Insofar as economics pretends to be the vehicle of human prosperity, and indeed of economic salvation, economics is a form of metaphysics and of eschatology. When all values are reduced to economic ones, when all human assets are accounted for in economic terms, economics becomes the ultimate matrix which gives meaning to human existence. In this sense economics becomes both metaphysics and eschatology. Alas, by elevating economics and industrial efficiency as our deities, we dwarf ourselves and suffer anguish as the result.

In the final reckoning, man cannot live by economic relations alone. The collapse of the Secular Imagination corresponds exactly to the collapse of economics as our ruling deity. This also signifies a collapse of the eschatological model which envisages the end of human life in terms of material satisfaction alone.

Secular Imagination is now digging its own graveyard. And our urgent question is: where do we now turn for replenishment and a new inspiration? We can turn to a new form of imagination, namely the transcendental imagination, and to a new eschatological model, which once again will be based on transcendental values and a new conception of man living in a symbiosis with the rest of the cosmos.

To say it once more: Man does not live by the strength of the relations of production (Marxism). Man lives by the strength of forms of consciousness, which he generates. Man as an evolutionary creature, is a consciousness-building animal, a mind-making animal, a sensitivity-generating animal. Through consciousness we have become human; by consciousness we live; toward greater consciousness we long and aspire; enlarged consciousness will be our salvation.

By creating new forms of consciousness we will re-connect man with other forms of life (in the all-encompassing frame of reverence for life), as well as reconnect Western man with other cultures and with himself. We have to be cautious for we have heard so many times that "new forms of consciousness will solve it all." Sometimes this message sounds glib. Yet, it has a meaning. For what else can counteract the malaise of our times? The internal reconstruction is much harder than any external reconstruction, for the latter can be done by machines, props, through other people. The internal reconstruction can be done only by each of us *alone*. This is the hard path. We in the West do not like this kind of path. Not only economists and politicians but all of us prefer salvation to come from outside—through external reconstruction, preferably through a technological fix.

We shall not be able to overcome Secular Imagination by tinkering with its symptoms only and by wallowing in its decadent substance (we love to wallow in our own decadence!). We can make a new start, but only by resorting to a new form of imagination—indeed *Imagination* as Blake conceived of it.

This new Transcendental Imagination and its consequences will be nothing short of a new religion. This religion, however, will not be rooted in past dogmas nor in past institutions, but will be based on a new comprehension of our unity with everything there is. It will be based on our reverence for life, which, in the ultimate analysis, is reverence for ourselves.

There is no escape from religion conceived in minimal terms, that is, as an eschatological frame of reference, within which the concept of the human life is justified and man's ultimate aspirations are acknowledged. We have a choice. We can choose a religion centered around the savage and limited gods called Technos and Economos that reduce our lives to their physical underpinnings, negate our transcendental values, and make the ultimate virtue of economic efficiency. Or we can endorse a religion based on compassion and transcendental visions of man's destiny, while man's horizons are continually unfolding to embrace the cosmos. The latter choice is the one we must make if we are to exercise our responsibility and our freedom: responsibility for the past and freedom to have a future. The drama of our future life is being played out now in the theatre of our minds.

22
The Promethean Heritage

Carl Jung had the courage to maintain—against the spirit
of progressive scientism of the early 20th century—that
myths are more sustaining to our lives than mere economic
security. We have increasingly come to recognize this
truth in recent years. If the meaning of human existence is
defined by man's spiritual life, then we can say that
man lives by myths alone. By myths I do not mean fables
and fairy tales but those towering symbols, embedded in the
religious and cultural substructure of people's lives,
which have the power to inspire and transform individuals
and societies alike.

Among those myths the Promethean story shines
supreme as it is the embodiment of evolution transforming itself. Prometheus, as we remember, stole the fire from
the gods and gave it to man. For this he was severely
punished by Zeus—by being chained to a rock, while
vultures ate his liver daily. The Greeks had a deep insight
into the nature of things: no great accomplishments without a sacrifice. However, the Promethean heritage must be
pursued in the right manner. We must take from
Prometheus what is most precious, illustrious, and enduring in him: his courage, his commitment, his responsibility, his altruism, his self-sacrifice; his realization that
the pursuit of progress must go hand in hand with the
awareness of hubris.

We must change our entire conception of man: away

from the Faustian man who is willing to sacrifice his
soul and everybody else for the sake of power; away from
the narcissistic man, who is totally absorbed in himself to
the exclusion of the entire world; and towards the new
Promethean man illumined and devoured by the new
Promethean fire. This image of man is in congruence with
evolution at large and with our own sense of our larger
destiny in the cosmos. Nothing was accomplished in evolution without a sacrifice. Evolution is a self-devouring
flame; and so must we be—to proceed to our higher
destinies.

We must be aware that the Promethean image has been
tarnished in past decades and centuries. The cyclops of
material progress has brutalized the sacred heritage
of spiritual fire. When we see the filthy, sulphurous
fumes that smell of death, we may be assured that they are
not the product of the Promethean fire but the residue
of the satanic mills. However, the dialectics of liberation
is painful and is abundant in pitfalls. By releasing
fire to man, Prometheus has unbound our destiny. Technological civilization has perverted the nature of this fire
and increasingly made it a fire of destruction. Thus
Prometheus has been re-bound. It is not the content of the
myth that is at fault but the narrow perspective of the
soulless prophets of material progress.

For Prometheus stands for the eternal myth of the
flaming imagination which is continually transcending its
own boundaries. Whenever we sacrifice ourselves for
the larger good of others, we are Promethean messengers.
And what would humanity be like without these Promethean messengers?

The new Promethean fire is the fire of imagination,
the ability to fly beyond, the challenge to our humanity
to be re-ignited, the realization of the full scope of
our courage and commitment, the determination of our
will to be like Prometheus—without whom we would
not have had fire nor many other enduring attributes
that make us human. The new Promethean commitment is not so much a great personal sacrifice but a

140

restatement of our human condition.

We have come from light and we shall return to light; for light is the beginning of it all and the purveyor of it all. Under the power of light have occurred the big cosmic transformations, which have gradually led us on. All the shapes of evolution have been but various stages in the transformation of light.

Yet the pain of creation and self-transcendence is always great, and sometimes excruciating. The last thing either Mozart or Beethoven deserved was to die in total misery. That geniuses like these or like Michelangelo suffered so terribly while bringing so much radiance to our lives epitomizes the beauty and the agony of the human condition. The agony of becoming! Those who transcend most must suffer most. Our little existential miseries should be seen in the right perspective. There is no inner transformation without some pain. No pain, no transformation, no progress.

There is yet another element in the Promethean story. While Prometheus is chained to the rock, vultures are eating away his liver. The vultures do not suffer, nor do they understand the suffering of Prometheus. One has indeed a choice: to be a vulture or a Prometheus, to try to live off others or to give unsparingly to others. We have been vultures often enough, if only inadvertently; when destiny offers each of us a choice to become a Prometheus (even on a small scale), we must rejoice in spite of the vultures around.

The verdicts of gods were inscrutable to the ancient Greeks. Nor should we think that everything is transparent in evolution. Day and night, darkness and light, radiance and suffering go together, at least in this imperfect, contingent world. To perform spiritedly, like a Prometheus, is one of the rare joys of human destiny.

23
Monod and Objectivity

The scientific world-view does not need any deity, so we are told. Yet objectivity has become the sacrosanct deity for the scientific mind—one of the unquestioned dogmas. I have already noted (in the introduction) that objectivity cannot be objectively justified. Yet the ideal of objectivity is one of the most important vehicles perpetuating the ideology of modern science. In fact, objectivity itself has become a part of the ideology of science. The interesting thing is that objectivity claims for itself the status of total impartiality, while it tries to bend our minds in a very one-sided direction. The issue of objectivity is very important, especially as the views of Jacques Monod (a Nobel laureate in biochemistry) are held in great esteem.

Monod has been one of the most articulate spokesmen for the objectivity of science, also one of the chief champions of the idea of chance and necessity as guiding and controlling the whole of evolution. In his opinion, science and its objectivity are sufficient instruments for the comprehension of evolution. Let us briefly consider Monod's conception of objectivity, which is the cornerstone of his conception of science. He writes (in *Chance and Necessity*, 1972, pp. 30, 31):

(i) "The cornerstone of the scientific method is the postulate that nature is objective.

(ii) "In other words, the *systematic* denial that 'true' knowledge can be reached by interpreting phenomena in terms of final causes—that is of 'purpose'.

(iii) "The postulate of objectivity is consubstantial with science,

(iv) "and has guided the *whole* of its prodigious development for three centuries.

(v) "It is impossible to escape it, even provisionally or in a limited area, without departing from the domain of science.

(vi) "Objectivity nevertheless obliges us to recognize the teleonomic character of living organisms. [*Teleonomic*, from *teleology*, the doctrine of final causes, the view that developments are due to purpose or design.]

(vii) "Here, therefore, at least in appearance, lies a profound epistemological contradiction."

Let us unravel the various contradictions and incoherences of Monod's position, and thereby show that even great scientists may talk nonsense when they apply themselves to problems lying outside their own province. When discussing philosophy and metaphysics, Monod did not know what he was talking about.

Is nature objective (i)? In a trivial sense, yes. By assuming certain attitudes (of separating some phenomena from other phenomena, and of examining these separated phenomena microscopically) we have been able to describe quite well certain *bits* of nature. Is this all there is to nature? Obviously not. For there are integrated wholes which science, so far, cannot describe. Moreover, there *may* be some other phenomena and relationships which are quite outside the understanding of science: if they do exist, we shall never find them through the existing apparatus of science, for science systematically excludes that which disagrees with its universe. So, the postulate of objectivity turns out to be either an unwarranted dogma— when it claims that nature is only that which science describes; or a very modest postulate indeed—when it claims that *certain* phenomena are the subject matter of physical science. In the latter case, our claim is so trivial that it is hardly worth mentioning.

By asserting (iii) that "the postulate of objectivity is

consubstantial with science," we only repeat a tautology or a dogma: a tautology if we define as scientific that which meets the requirements of the postulate of objectivity (whatever way we define the postulate of objectivity); a dogma if we insist that all valid knowledge is science and that all science must be based on the postulate of objectivity.

Monod seems to have given only one specific formulation of the postulate of objectivity, namely (ii) that no "true" knowledge can be reached by interpreting phenomena in terms of final causes. So objectivity comes to as much and as little as the denial of final causes, of Master Plans, of teleology. Science is then defined in a negative way; as that which denies final causes. This is a very modest claim indeed and certainly not sufficient to make objectivity, so conceived, the basis of all science, present or historical.

Even this modest claim is marred by some misconceptions. For it is not the case that no true knowledge can be acquired by resorting to final causes and teleology. True knowledge, as Popper has demonstrated, can be acquired in all sorts of ways. Anything can be a source of knowledge. We must not confuse the sources of our knowledge, which are exceedingly numerous, with the justification of knowledge, and especially with the justification of scientific knowledge. Even if we are generous to Monod and grant him that there is such a thing as objectivity, which we might identify with the ontological structure of the universe which physics assumes and then explores, we are bound to deny that this postulate has guided the prodigious development of science during the last three centuries. The development of science has been guided by all sorts of principles, not the least important of which was the idea of Master Plan, or the purposeful arrangement of nature by an Omnipotent Being—which we have seen in Copernicus and Newton—an idea which Monod most anxiously wishes to expel from the domain of science. And the history of science will not support Monod either in his contention that it is impossible

144

to escape the principle of objectivity without departing from the domain of science itself. Science is a messy affair, and all kinds of principles and devices are used to get *results*; take, for instance, the process of the discovery of DNA as described by Watson. Monod's claim could be made valid if and only if objectivity is defined as *everything that goes on in science*. Then the postulate of objectivity is so all-embracing that it becomes meaningless.

We encounter even greater difficulties with (vi). This very "objectivity nevertheless obliges us to recognize the teleonomic character of living organisms." Why? In what way? From the principle of objectivity it does *not* follow logically that we have to recognize the teleonomic character of living organisms. Teleonomy does not follow from objectivity. Full stop. We have to recognize the teleonomic character of living organisms only when we recognize *living* organisms, and especially when we recognize their evolution. There is a large leap between objectivity as pursued in the domain of physics and the teleonomic character of living organisms, particularly viewed in their evolution.

The profound epistemological contradiction which Monod mentions in (vii) only arises when we accept the postulate of objectivity and the rigid deterministic physical model that goes with it, and then find ourselves (on the grounds of the accepted epistemology) unable to account for the phenomenon of life, and particularly the phenomenon of evolution. But we can easily resolve Monod's epistemological contradiction—by dissolving the alleged universality of the principle of objectivity. After such a dissolution science will not fall, nor will the universe collapse.

Does my critique of objectivity negate the value of science? Not at all. The creation of science was one of the glories of the human mind. But objectivity must not be worshipped like a goddess; for it is only one of the many sensitivities we have developed. Newtonian physics and its conception of objectivity has been *one* of the forms of understanding of the world—an invented form through

145

which we have been receiving the world in a specific way.

The concept of objectivity of Newtonian physics was, in actual fact, a specific product of the Newtonian comprehension of the world. In the course of the development of the physical paradigm, in the course of the development of the mechanistic model, that is, objectivity—as a specific capacity of the human mind—became one of the forms of our sensitivities: dry, abstract, quantitative.

Objectivity as an attribute of our cognitive apparatus is not given to us from the cradle. On the contrary, it is imposed on us in the course of learning, is the result of a specific process of conditioning after which we *become* objective in our thought and perception. This happens particularly after we have spent a number of years in a laboratory continuously attempting to verify and justify the objective method of describing the world. Thus objectivity *is* a form of sensitivity. Through objectivity we are receiving and reading the world in a specific way, specific for Newtonian physics; we are in fact transforming or co-creating the world within the model of Newtonian mechanics. However, the Newtonian world-view is not one based on common sense; it is based on Newton's metaphysical assumptions.

Other forms of sensitivity (as we have discussed earlier) enable us to receive and transform the world according to different models. When we talk about the reception of the world through our sensitivity, we have in mind not only our brain but the entire human being within whom all evolution is contained. The eye perceives, the nervous system interprets, the mind formulates the perceptions in accordance with the endowment of the species; and within the human species in accordance with the principles of the culture by which a given person has been formed and conditioned. The act of perception itself, the act of "visual" contact with the world, contains more than speech can express. This act itself embodies many forms of sensitivity which are beyond intellectual categories of the brain. The act of perception is unitary, holistic, and complete; its intellectual deciphering is partial and abstract, always a contrived process. The perception of one solitary oak standing in its glory in the middle of a meadow is an experience of delight beyond any linguistic description. Objectivity is good for the laboratory. But laboratories often lobotomize our minds. For full living we need a solitary oak, standing in the middle of the meadow with which we can enter into communion.

24
The Cosmic Laws

Objectivity is not an intellectual deity! We must not worship idols; we must guard ourselves against any form of deification of human understanding. One of them—at the other end of the spectrum from objectivity—is the idea of *cosmic laws* which govern it all.

The living universe is not governed by immutable laws. If there are any laws in evolution, these laws are not absolute. The conception of a law, established once and for all, is in contradiction with evolution envisaged as transcending itself. If evolution is emergent, new articulations and new laws governing its being are inevitable. Absolute laws would signify stagnation and petrification. There is one immutable law, in nature, in evolution and in the cosmos: mutability. "The nature of the laws of nature changes." (Prigogine)

The structure of DNA could have been different. The structure of our comprehension could have been different. The shape of our culture—if the Persians and not the Greeks had emerged victorious at the turn of the 5th century B.C.—would have been different; hundreds of other things in our make-up could have been different.

But the universe is not whimsical. We are not mere puppets without coherence. There are certain tendencies and propensities in the existing structure of the cosmos. There are certain laws of evolutionarily change. Certain developments led contingently to other developments.

There is "good karma" and there is "bad karma," and there are the consequences of each. But there isn't an absolute law that governs it all. You don't need to use the term "karma" in order to know that there are cumulative consequences of our actions, that all things are causally connected, that you sometimes trigger off new chains of reactions.

If evolution is emergent there cannot be an absolute law. Yes, there are some tendencies and propensities, general principles, so to speak, according to which things are transformed. Principles are not absolute or cosmic laws. They only commit you to the recognition of cause and effect in your own life and in the life of the universe. They do not force you to acknowledge an iron necessity built into it all. What kind of laws the cosmos is governed by may be entirely beyond our comprehension; nor should we presume that there is such a set of laws. Why should there be? We live in a creative, open, participatory universe. If this is so, then there is no necessity for cosmic laws. Let us reiterate. If evolution is creative, emergent, and self-transcendent, then it cannot be clad in any iron law, for its mutations and new transformations are its main modus operandi.

Yet, some conceive of the cosmic law as more fundamental than evolution itself. In their minds God established a structure and a set of mechanisms from which all springs, by which all moves, and to which all will return. Such is the legacy of many religions. This legacy is important, for it helps the human race in articulating itself in spiritual terms. But this legacy must now be viewed as history, not as a living substance. For this legacy now makes evolution incoherent. By saying, or at least implying, that there is an iron-clad blueprint, we are denying (at least implicitly) the creative, open, and emergent nature of evolution.

There is no need to clutch at the straw of absolute laws, even if one wants to believe in a personal God. The personal God is the God within, through which we articulate divinity in ourselves and in evolution. "Cosmic law" is shorthand for the idea of the transformation of matter into spirit, a metaphor rather than a law.

Great prophets and spiritual leaders of the past, such as Moses and Zoroaster, conceived of the universe as a gigantic cosmic order with inexhaustible sources of energy and knowledge in it. Man's harmonious path, or his living according to the law, is his understanding of the web and his ability to weave himself into this great cosmic canvas from which he derives support and nourishment. The forces which work in favor of human beings on the path of self-perfectibility were called angels by Moses and his followers. All the links connecting man's consciousness with "angels" can be conceived as the domain of the cosmic law. Therefore, there is a place for one cosmic law (which can be identified with God) as long as we bear in mind that what we call "God" or the "cosmic law" is a way of endowing symbolic significance to the natural forces of evolution which resolve themselves in those fields of energy/consciousness we know as culture, spirituality, and religion.

25
Of Plato, Kant, and the New Cosmological Unity

One of the great questions of Western philosophy has been: How can we secure simultaneously the objectivity of knowledge and the reliability of morals, so that our mind moves in the universe of order while our heart dwells in the universe of compassion? The universe of compassion must not be considered merely subjective, but one that is grounded in a larger design of the cosmos. Both the order of the mind and the order of the heart must have common cosmic underpinnings.

Plato's answer to this dilemma was to invent the Forms, absolute, everlasting, imperishable, which underlie the existence of all objects and of all virtue. For him all learning is but the recognition by the soul of that knowledge which is possessed before it became embodied. When the soul is incarnate, "it is contaminated with imperfection of our body"; it then partially forgets the knowledge it originally possessed but is reminded of this by the earthly copies of the Form. Thus all knowledge is "remembering" (*anamnesis*). Everything that we learn is the unveiling of what we have known, is the lifting up of the clouds of obscurity brought about by our senses and our bodily entrapments, so that the soul can see again. Right knowledge means, for Plato, the recognition of the whole plan of creation, including our place in it—our duties and responsibilities. By recognizing the true nature of the world, the soul recognizes the path of the "right life" and the place of virtue in it.

The objectivity of morals and the reliability of man's knowledge are achieved through the same means: the soul's apprehension of the underlying Forms—which are the guarantors of the order of being external to man and also guarantors of the moral order.

Twenty-two centuries after Plato, Emmanuel Kant addressed himself to the same cardinal problem: How can we secure objectivity of morals and reliability of knowledge? But he found that there are different grounds for securing each. The moral law was to be grounded in the sovereignty of man, which is unique and independent of the physical universe. Kant found objective grounds for reliable knowledge in the fixed structure of the mind, which, through its unalterable and permanent categories (imposed on the world), makes the world comply to the order of the mind.

Kant's discovery that the mind shapes reality according to its own structure was such a revelation to him that he called it "the second Copernican Revolution." Indeed, if we compare him with Plato, we realize that the entire anchor was moved—from the Forms, existing independently of the mind, to the mind itself, in which these Forms, under the guise of categories, reside. Thus the order of knowledge is not guaranteed by the Forms (existing independently of the mind) but by the very structure of the mind.

Yet there remained this other problem: what to do with human morality, which Kant did not wish to subsume under the mechanistic laws of science. So he declared that morality remains in the sovereignty of the individual and is governed by the uniquely human moral imperative, whose briefest formulation is: Never treat another human being simply as a means but always as an end. Kant's overall design could be formulated as follows: the starry heaven above you—as structured by the mind and grasped by the laws of science; and the moral law within you—as guided by the moral imperative.

Two centuries after Kant, we must address the same

dilemma. For as the result of the reign of empiricism we have inherited a shattered world in which everything is in pieces, with "all coherence gone." We must again bring some coherence to the world. To attempt to bring a new coherence is not only a requirement of the mind, which cannot cope with the universe of incoherence and chaos; more importantly, it is an existential necessity of man who must *belong*, as otherwise he feels alienated and paranoid. The needs of coherence and belonging are among basic needs of man; their satisfaction is just as important as the satisfaction of the need for shelter and food. On the spiritual level—belonging is our shelter, coherence is our food.

Plato attempted to establish the unity of knowledge and morals by going *downward*; by connecting things with the underlying Forms. Within the evolutionary model we are establishing this unity by going *upward*: by observing how the process of becoming molds the varieties of being into new ontological and spiritual forms.

Evolution, conceived as the articulation of becoming as it passes into being, can be presented by a series of screens which show the process of crystallization of latent potentialities into actual states of being. Becoming is the passage from non-being into being. The attributes through which being articulates itself are, so to speak, visible flowers of the tree of becoming.

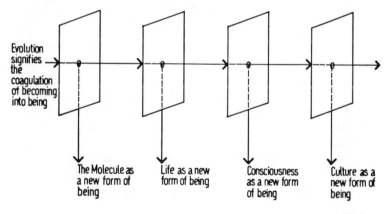

Evolution signifies the coagulation of becoming into being

The Molecule as a new form of being

Life as a new form of being

Consciousness as a new form of being

Culture as a new form of being

In the absence of the Form "out there," which is the anchor of our morals, how should we think about the "roots" of our morality? The term *roots* may be inappropriate, for it evokes something solid, rooted to the ground. How should we think about the foundations of our morality, then? Again the term *foundations* is loaded as it presupposes some immovable ground—very much in the image of Plato's Form. Morality conceived as evolutionary unfolding could be thought of as the flowering of a flower. The roots are necessary for the flower to be nourished. But the roots do not blossom; only the flower does—when all the conditions for its unfolding are right.

Morality conceived as the flowering of the human species simply means that, in the process of its becoming, the species acquired the sensitivities that enabled it, through its individuals, to act as responsible moral agents. The tender flower of morality blossoms only in the right conditions, like a delicate and demanding flower. To make these conditions right, we have to insure that the process of becoming is correctly articulated, that is to say that it unfolds by producing the sensitivity called the moral sense. Thus the right process of becoming is the guarantor of our morality.

The essence of being is a time-induced articulation of becoming. Evolution is becoming which continually explodes into being. The forms of being are the flowers of becoming. In the very idea of being, which comes to existence through the *articulation* of becoming, we find the underlying objectivity for both morals and knowledge.

On the level of knowledge, the right articulation of our mind leads to the sensitivity called conceptual thinking and furthermore critical thinking. They form together the canvas for the acquisition and screening of knowledge. Indeed our knowledge is that which this canvas (the special conceptual sensitivity of the mind) is capable of accommodating.

There is thus a unity between the real and the moral, as Plato postulated. But it is on a different level and in a different framework from what Plato had thought. The

154

process of articulation of evolution is the guarantor of the validity of the forms of life; it is also the guarantor of objectivity of morals and the reliability of knowledge, which are not merely subjective but have some ratification in nature, in the way things are.

In this evolutionary process of articulation we must not forget the role of the interactive mind. This interactive mind is the expression of the sum total of the sensitivities which went into its making, as already discussed. These sensitivities are filters through which mind views and receives reality. Mind is *within* reality and, at the same time, *of* the reality that surrounds it. Like the light within, it illumines reality; by illuminating, it articulates; by articulating, it co-creates.

Let us represent: Mind I—mind in the narrow sense; Mind II—the subtotal of all sensitivities of which Mind I is made; Mind III—reality, within which both Mind I and Mind II reside. These are shown as three concentric spheres (I, II, and III) each merging with the next and each an aspect of the other two. Mind I or the discursive mind, is what is usually called the brain, the agency for abstract cerebration, epitomized by logical thinking. Mind II includes intuition, thinking through the eyes, and all other sensitivities which make us *know*, in the various senses of the term. Mind III is the ultimate extension of Mind I and Mind II as they interact with "the stuff of the universe" and transform it into what we think we know.

To say that *reality* is a form of mind may strike some as an unjustified semantic liberty, but it is not. As mind is part of the real, so reality is part of the mind.

Sphere I and sphere III are aspects of each other. Consider the statement: "The symmetry of this pale pink carnation is a beautiful phenomenon." Insofar as our carnation is a "phenomenon," it belongs to the sphere of reality (sphere III). Insofar as it is "symmetrical," "pale pink," and "beautiful," it belongs to the sphere of mind (spheres I, II). Insofar as we make a verbal utterance about it, it belongs to the sphere of the discursive mind (sphere I). Insofar as we appreciate its total beauty, it belongs to the

155

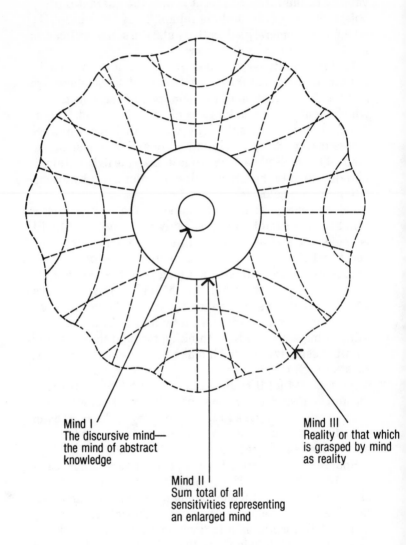

Mind I
The discursive mind—
the mind of abstract
knowledge

Mind II
Sum total of all
sensitivities representing
an enlarged mind

Mind III
Reality or that which
is grasped by mind
as reality

sphere of sensitivities (Mind II). Each of our statements about reality transcends this reality, for reality itself belongs to the sphere of the mind.

Sphere III (reality) is mind, but not in the same sense in which sphere I is mind. True. However, *within the sphere of reality itself we can hardly find two different things which are real in the same sense.*

The diagram showing the three spheres merging into each other is meant to convey the essential *evolutionary* unity of our cosmology. Mind I and Mind III are aspects of each other but at the same time exhibit different stages and different modes of the articulation of evolution. Mind I, being of more recent origin, incorporates Mind III which has provided the material for the making of Mind I; but Mind I, in turn, makes *human* sense of Mind III.

Our language, dominated by the precepts of empiricism, is recalcitrant in allowing us to express the new cosmological unity, which clearly goes against its grain. I shall therefore call on poets.

William Blake says:

> But to the eye of the man of Imagination,
> Nature is Imagination itself.
> AS MAN IS, SO HE SEES.

The 13th century Persian poet, Mahmud Shabistari, expresses similar insights:

> The world has become a man, and man a world.
> There is no clearer explanation than this.
> When you look well into the root of the matter,
> He is at once seen, seeing eye, and things seen.

The poet E. E. Cummings says: "Always the more beautiful answer who asks the more difficult question." Instead of asking ourselves petty questions in an outmoded frame of reference—for empiricism *is* an outmoded frame of reference—we must have the courage to ask ourselves new bold questions, for in their significance

157

lies our salvation. The question which I have been asking myself is: Can we hope to develop a new unitary cosmology, one which would be so conceived that it renders the universe as home for man; which would provide the basis for our reconciliation with nature, as well as resolve the contradictory aspects of present scientific knowledge; and which at the same time would provide an outline of a new theory of mind? The answer is: Yes. This answer, when articulated, means a new cosmology, a new conception of mind, and a new conception of reality.*

In this chapter I addressed myself to the role of the mind in the universe of becoming. *The becoming of the universe is inseparable from the becoming of the mind.* This insight is in perfect harmony with the new ontological vistas unveiled to us by present particle physics, which has abandoned the rigid, deterministic Newtonian framework, and which came to recognize that—on the ultimate level of analysis—the observer and the observed merge inseparably.

Let me draw some general conclusions. There is no *objective* reality in the absolute sense, as there is no such thing as objectivity independent of our cognitive faculties. We do not photograph this (purportedly objective) reality in our scientific theories. We can break the whole process into three components: the reality out there; the process of photographing it; and the process of developing the negatives, that is to say the process of formulation of theories and of knowledge. These three are aspects of each other, cannot be torn from each other, as they co-define and co-constitute each other. The nature of our mind is the nature of our knowledge is the nature of our reality. (Try to be an amoeba and "think" what your 'knowledge' and what your 'reality' would be like.)

I am aware that I am proposing some rather uncomfortable notions. But the history of modern science has

---

*See also my book: *Eco-Philosophy, Designing New Tactics for Living*, Boston, Marion Boyars, 1981, especially Chap. 3.

been but the story of uncomfortable and improbable notions that have become subsequently built into the floor of our understanding of 'reality'. Ours is the universe of becoming: the universe of emergent qualities, the universe of new forms of understanding, which, although they at first appear as conceptual shocks, after a time resolve themselves as new illuminating insights into the nature of things.

In every culture there is an intimate unity between the concept of reality, the concept of knowledge, and the concept of the mind. The three are bound together in a triangular co-defining relationship. This can also be observed in Western culture of the past three centuries. If we contrast classical physics with present physics, we can present them by two triangles.

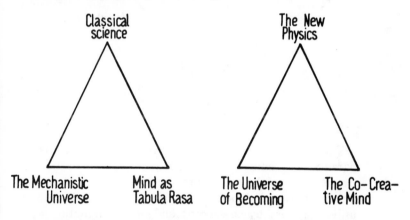

Within the empiricist tradition the mind is conceived as Tabula Rasa—a clean sheet of paper on which experience does all the work. There is a congruence between the static and dead universe that empiricism postulates and its concept of static, entirely passive mind. With the rediscovery of the universe of becoming, which the new physics supports in a variety of ways, the role of the mind of necessity must be redefined.

We should be aware that in our day and age the two triangles co-exist in the world of thought, but in a rather confused way, which is causing—through the

159

discrepancies they generate—a great deal of conceptual stress and quite a bit of intellectual paranoia, to say nothing of the forsaken sense of belonging.

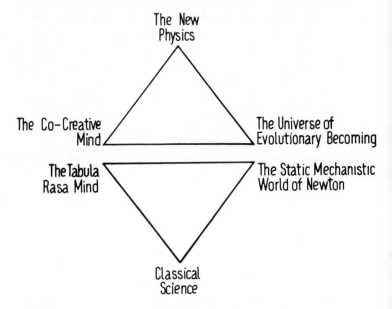

The ecological theory of mind wants to remove this paranoia as it encourages us to take possession of the new freedom in which, unanchored from the shores of determinism, we shall be floating through the new unfolding universe; aided by new Transcendental Imagination we shall discover new forms of understanding of which philosophers and scientists have never dreamed in their narrowly conceived rational ivory towers of academia.

The emergence of mind is one of the lasting mysteries. To conceive of mind as a mystery is less mysterious and less mystifying than to hold that the mind is a mere brain working according to physiological, mechanistic laws alone; for it is to admit that mystery is part of the natural order of things. Mind and imagination are bound together. The nature of imagination gives us a more penetrating clue to the understanding of the mind than a hundred

neuro-physiological studies. The nature of imagination
is wonderfully mysterious. And wonderfully mysterious is
the quality of the universe that mind/imagination render
to us. The world, the mind, and the human being are
always given together. As the astrophysicist John
Archibald Wheeler says: "The universe does not exist 'out
there' independent of us. We are inescapably involved
in bringing about that which appears to be happening. We
are not only observers. We are participators. In some
strange sense this is a *participatory universe*." To participate is to contribute. To participate is to be responsible.
Responsibility, as an attribute of our humanity, merges
with the intoxicating freedom which we inherit once
we allow our participatory and co-creative mind to unfold
by unfolding new layers and new aspects of reality.

26
Glory to Evolution

Glory to Evolution! As it unfolds itself it creates us. As
we are created, we unfold it further.

Evolution is not blind; nor is it subject to rigid, deterministic laws. It is a process of continuous articulation.
Each articulation is a process of creation. After it has
occurred, the world has changed—become richer.

And so it is with the articulation of our minds. Each
articulation changes us in the process. By articulating ourselves we, like flowers, come to fruition. We realize our
potential by articulating ourselves: on the biological plane,
on the intellectual plane, on the cosmic or spiritual plane.

We shall need to develop new forms of sensitivity. We
shall need more love: to give and to receive. We shall
need to be nourished by new springs of imagination which
illumine and transform, which give rise to new sensitivities
of thought and of feelings.

The road will be long and arduous. It will entail much
pain for every articulation and every creation, for the effort
of overcoming the inertia of existing things is painful.
Every new articulation is another aspect of the Promethean
story. The joy of unfolding and the pain of sacrifice are
inseparable. But there is a glory in this pain and arduous-
ness: the glory of bringing the dim radiance in us to a
greater radiance. Our freedom is to make the right choice;
our necessity is to accept the divine. "Who rightly with
necessity complies in things divine, we count him

skilled and wise." (Euripides)

What of happiness then? Of human happiness, that is, which we all crave? Happiness comes uninvited when we are *ready* for it. How can we make ourselves ready for it? By not striving consciously to possess it. Therefore, we should not strive for happiness. We can only arrive at happiness while striving for other things. Happiness is not a fixed state of being; it is a state of perpetual becoming. Happiness cannot be designed. When happiness arrives, we are no longer conscious of striving for it.

What should we strive for? The meaning of life, the fulfillment that goes beyond our individual egoistic self. We are as great as the causes we aspire to. Great causes elevate us and make us transcend our small self. Great causes pervade us with reverence and infuse us with dignity, which are necessary components of a worthy life. We must stretch ourselves to the maximum in the service of others, in the cause of altruism—merge with the larger scheme of things by understanding that human destiny is made of the stars and not only of ordinary clay. And then our life will be enhanced, our being enlarged. And perhaps as a byproduct we will arrive at happiness.

What is happiness? Not a state of sensual satisfaction or titillating physical comfort, but a state of inner radiance which will be recognized more and more as we approach it. Happiness is being at peace with ourselves, while the self is united with a larger order of things.

The truly blessed people, the giants of human thought and spirit, such as Gandhi, Albert Schweitzer, or Mother Teresa of Calcutta, did not search for happiness. Yet we find their lives radiant and inspiring—full to the brim in the service of great causes, in the service of others, in the service of large ideals which alone make sense of human destinies.

The concept of happiness should be abandoned, for it is usually a trap concealing an ego trip. The path to happiness is to lose our ego and ambition and to acquire a vision and a mission. Both the vision and mission must be congruent with the evolutionary unfolding. For there is nothing outside the bounds of evolution.

Glory to evolution, for it is God. God is evolution realizing itself; transforming us into more and more radiant fragments of godliness. We are God in the making. We learn the meaning of God in the process of becoming one. "In truth who knows God becomes God" (*Mandukya Upanishad*). The terror of this realization must not be a license for arrogance but an invitation to humility. Let us seek light while we are aware of the darkness around us. Let us celebrate life while we are aware of the agony of its becoming. Let us embrace God while we are aware that at present we are only human. O, let us live in joy, in light among those who grope in darkness.

Index

human life, 61. *See also*
Language as transcendence

Vienna Circle, 104
Von Bertalanffy, Ludwig, 119

Watson, J. B., 104
Wheeler, John Archibald, 161
Wholeness, 93-94; in
Hippocrates, 91

More Quest books on Evolution

Basic Ideas of Occult Wisdom
By Anna Kennedy Winner
With one chapter devoted to
our progressive development

Being, Evolution and Immortality
By Haridas Chaudhuri
The Occidental world discovers
the miracle of spiritual evolution

The Christening of Karma
By Geddes MacGregor
Evolution and karma as
part of Christian scripture

Culture, Crisis and Creativity
By Dane Rudhyar
Evolution as transcendence—
from crisis to creativity

The Evolution of Integral Consciousness
By Haridas Chaudhuri
Our awareness as a holistic,
developmental phenomenon

**Available from:
QUEST BOOKS
306 West Geneva Road
Wheaton, Illinois 60189**